TREASURY AUCTION RESULTS AS INTEREST RATE PREDICTORS

JAMES ALAN LARSON

GARLAND PUBLISHING, INC.
NEW YORK & LONDON / 1994

Library of Congress Cataloging-in-Publication Data

Larson, James Alan, 1948–
    Treasury auction results as interest rate predictors / James Alan
Larson.
        p.   cm. — (The Financial sector of the American economy)
    Includes index.
    ISBN 0–8153–1682–8 (alk. paper)
    1. Interest rates—United States—Forecasting.   2. Government
securities—United States.   I. Title.   II. Series.
HG1623.U5L37   1994
332.63'232—dc20   93–41567
                                                            CIP

Printed on acid-free, 250-year-life paper
Manufactured in the United States of America

DEDICATION

This work is dedicated to my friend, Alan Kavie - may he rest in peace.

CONTENTS

FINDINGS (Cont.)

FOREWORD

Forecasting future market movements is an occupation as old as markets themselves. With the extreme volatility in interest rates experienced during the late 1970s and early 1980s, the need for an accurate interest rate forecasting methodology became extremely important.

The purpose of this study was to determine if U.S. Treasury auction results could be helpful in the production of accurate interest rate forecasts.

In answering this question two specific Treasury issues were studied: the five-year note and thirty-year bond. The results of the study indicate that the use of five-year auction data are of limited usefulness in forecasting future interest rates. One can theorize that this is the case because the five-year sector of the U.S. Treasury market is more efficient than the thirty-year sector.

Data on the thirty-year auction are much more useful from a forecasting perspective. Analysis of the coverage ratio indicates that large coverage ratios are often associated with falling interest rates. Of greater interest is the fact that when "primary dealers" purchase large portions of the thirty-year bond, relative to the amount they bid for, bond prices typically erode forcing interest rates higher. Theoretically, this phenomenon occurs because dealers have effectively satisfied their demand for the security in the auction process and thus the lack of follow-through buying allows prices to drop and rates to rise. This result also lends credence to the argument that the thirty-year sector of the Treasury market is less efficient than the five-year sector.

Finally, during this research no evidence of collusion among primary dealers was discovered. It is this researcher's opinion that much of the concern on this subject deals with misconceptions about the actual definition of the term.

PREFACE

The securities markets are an extremely interesting and exciting area of study. Events can occur down the street or on the other side of the globe and have immediate impact on securities prices.

The fixed income market specifically felt the impact of both domestic and international events during the decade of the 1980s. The research effort discussed throughout the first five chapters of this book were directed toward that specific time frame.

Following the decade of the 80s, however several significant fixed income market events occurred which were also very noteworthy. In the interests of exploring these events thoroughly the reader will find the sixth chapter of this book entitled "Recent Events" very enlightening.

In this chapter the reader will find a thorough discussion of the Salomon Brothers bidding scandal, potential primary dealer collusion, recent experiments in U.S. Treasury auction techniques and other major Treasury market and auction reforms.

Upon completion of the entire six chapters, readers will possess a thorough understanding of both the historical perspective of this study as well as knowledge relating to the most recent market events.

ACKNOWLEDGMENTS

I would like to take this opportunity to thank the following individuals for their valuable aid, guidance and support in the preparation of this study:

Dr. Barry Heermann
Dr. Robert L. Johnson
Dr. Abe Harraf
Dr. Brian Nordstrom
Mr. Fred Landry
Mrs. Elaine Kramer

I would also like to thank my wife, Karen, for her help and understanding as this study was being undertaken.

ILLUSTRATIONS

INTRODUCTION

Uncertainty is a salient feature of security investment. Economic forces are not understood well enough for predictions to be beyond doubt or error. Even if the consequences of economic conditions were understood perfectly, non-economic influences can change the course of general prosperity, the level of the market or the success of a particular security. The health of the President, changes in international tensions, increases or decreases in military spending, an extremely dry summer, the success of an invention, the miscalculation of a business manager - any of these events as well as many others can affect the capital gains or dividends of securities.

The paragraph above is paraphrased from Harry Markowitz's classic work entitled "Portfolio Selection and Efficient Diversification of Investments" (Markowitz 1959, 4). Although written in 1959 and directed primarily toward equity investing, these statements could have easily described the scenario encountered in the fixed-income markets during more recent times. An updated version of Mr. Markowitz's observation might include additional factors such as current and prospective rates of inflation, Federal Reserve monetary policy, government fiscal policy, U. S. Treasury debt management policies, and the relative supply and demand for funds.

The latter portion of the 1970s and the decade of the 1980s, by most measures, was one of the most volatile and treacherous in recent bond market history. As the 1970s drew to a close, events were unfolding that contributed to this turbulence. Inflation was certainly one key supporting factor. Inflation, for purposes of this study, shall be defined as a "rising general level of prices." Most economists distinguish between two types of inflation: demand-pull and cost-push inflation. These two types of inflation are *not* unrelated or mutually exclusive, and most economists would agree that during this era both types were operative (McConnell 1987, 179).

1

As is evident through a perusal of Table 1, the five year average inflation rate underwent substantial upward pressure between the early portion of the 1960s and the last half of the 1970s.

TABLE 1

U.S. ANNUAL CPI INFLATION RATES FIVE YEAR AVERAGES: 1960-79	
PERIOD	AVERAGE INFLATION RATE
1960-64	1.2%
1965-69	3.4%
1970-74	6.1%
1975-79	8.2%

Source: Petersen, 1989, 57.

The upsurge in inflation is even more dramatic if calendar year annual rates of change in consumer prices are examined as depicted in Table 2. As this table shows, after registering a 4.8 percent rate of gain in 1976, each successive yearly rate reached higher levels, peaking at 13.3 percent in 1979.

Although clearly a problem, inflation was *not* the only factor contributing to this unstable environment. Other contributory forces included a monetary policy which had allowed monetary aggregate growth rates, as defined by M1, to grow at a 10 percent annual rate of gain during the first three quarters of 1979 (Heyne 1991, 499). Other contributory events included the following: 1) new monetary operating procedures adopted by the Federal Reserve in October 1979, 2) announcement of new money supply definitions in February 1980, 3) imposition of credit controls in March 1980 and 4) passage of banking deregulation in March 1980 (Cargill 1991, 281).

TABLE 2

CONSUMER PRICE INDEX ANNUAL RATES OF CHANGE	
YEAR	CPI CHANGE
1976	+4.8%
1977	+6.8%
1978	+9.0%
1979	+13.3%

Source: Ibbotson 1989, 187.

Superimposed on this backdrop was the 1980 election of Ronald Reagan which led to a series of individual income tax cuts combined with an enormous build up in defense spending. This resulted in an explosion in the unified federal deficit as is depicted in Table 3. The unified federal budget deficit grew at an astonishing compound annual growth rate of 27.5 percent from 1979-1986.

The growth in deficit spending led to explosive growth in the issuance of U.S. Treasury bills, notes and bonds to finance the shortfall (See Table 4). It took the United States 205 years to accrue its first trillion dollars of debt and only *FIVE* years to accrue its second trillion (Wallace 1985, 92). Equally startling is the growth in debt per capita which is also displayed in Table 4. During the same time period debt per person in the U.S. grew from $3,639 to $11,402, a compound- annual growth rate of 12.1 percent. Even after adjusting for inflation, the *real* compound annual rate of increase is 6.3 percent.

Not only is the absolute magnitude of debt a concern, but many market participants question the ability of foreigners, particularly the Japanese, to continue to absorb ever-increasing quantities of Treasury debt. Blustein points out that the Japanese were net purchasers of $50 billion of U.S. stocks and bonds during calendar year 1986. By 1990 however, it is estimated that this same important investor group will be net *sellers* of $10 billion in U.S. securities (Blustein 1990, H6).

TABLE 3

UNIFIED FEDERAL BUDGET (DEFICIT) SELECTED YEARS	
FISCAL YEAR	DEFICIT (BILLIONS $)
1979	(40.2)
1980	(73.8)
1981	(78.9)
1982	(127.9)
1983	(207.8)
1984	(185.3)
1985	(212.3)
1986	(221.2)

Source: First Boston Corporation 1990, 42.

While this upsurge in inflation, deficit spending and Treasury financing was occurring, the fixed income markets were feeling the effects. Although research has been unable to specifically link these factors to interest rate movements, the data presented in Table 5 are self-explanatory. Beginning in 1977, interest rates on government securities began an incessant march to ever higher levels. Although only five year and thirty year constant maturities are depicted in Table 5, the same trend persisted across the yield curve. Using these yield- curve segments for illustration, the absolute level of rates *more than doubled* on five year maturities between 1977-1981. Although rates fell sharply between 1981-83, they surged again in 1984 before dropping precipitously during 1985 and 1986. An upturn then resumed during 1987-88.

TABLE 4

TOTAL INTEREST BEARING PUBLIC DEBT SECURITIES		
END OF FISCAL YEAR	BILLIONS $	$ PER CAPITA
1979	819.007	3639
1980	906.402	3980
1981	996.495	4330
1982	1140.883	4907
1983	1375.751	5859
1984	1559.570	6580
1985	1821.010	7610
1986	2212.684	9158
1987	2347.750	9624
1988	2599.877	10555
1989	2836.309	11402

Source: Council of Economic Advisors 1991, 321, 351 & 384.

It is interesting to note in Table 5 that CPI inflation rates peaked at 13.5 percent per annum in 1980 and rose at decreasing rates of gain through 1983. On the other hand, interest rates continued to rise dramatically into 1981. This relationship gave rise to exceedingly high *real inflation adjusted rates* of interest as depicted in Table 6. This again underlines the fact that forces *other than* inflation were driving interest rates during this era.

Given the significant level of volatility noted in Tables 5 and 6, a few words of clarification may be in order regarding fixed-income securities. Bonds or fixed-income securities possess two distinct features that are not found in equity securities. First, they are readily classified into clear-cut groups. Second, there exists a generally accepted yardstick for measuring the value of a given fixed income security; namely yield to maturity. This yield to maturity measurement tool can be used to depict the overall level of rates and the spreads between securities as well as the bid-offer spread of a single security (Levine 1975, 226).

TABLE 5

COMPARISON OF U.S. TREASURY BOND YIELDS and CPI INFLATION 1977-1988 (IN PERCENT)			
CALENDAR YEAR	5 YEAR CONSTANT MATURITY*	LONG TERM CONSTANT MATURITY*	ΔCPI
1977	6.99	7.06	6.5
1978	8.32	7.89	7.6
1979	9.52	8.74	11.3
1980	11.48	10.81	13.5
1981	14.24	12.87	10.3
1982	13.01	12.23	6.2
1983	10.80	10.84	3.2
1984	12.24	11.99	4.3
1985	10.13	10.75	3.6
1986	7.31	8.14	1.9
1987	7.94	8.64	3.6
1988	8.47	8.98	4.1

* Bond yields are annual averages of monthly data.
Sources: U. S. Bureau of the Census 1990 p.468 & 510.
U. S. Bureau of the Census 1986, 506.

TABLE 6

| REAL INTEREST RATES 1977-87 (IN PERCENT) ||
CALENDAR YEAR	T-BILL RATE MINUS INFLATION
1977	(1.5)
1978	(1.7)
1979	(2.6)
1980	(1.0)
1981	5.3
1982	6.4
1983	4.8
1984	5.7
1985	3.8
1986	5.0
1987	1.0

Source: Ibbotson, 1989, 195.

Equation 1 below displays the mathematical relationship between bond pricing and the yield-to-maturity calculation. As shown, the value of any given fixed-income security can be obtained by summing the present value of all future coupon payments with the present value of the lump sum payment due at maturity.

EQUATION 1

$$V=\sum_{t=1}^{2n} \frac{I}{2}(\frac{1}{1+\frac{k_d}{2}})^t+M(\frac{1}{1+\frac{k_d}{2}})^{2n}$$

where I = annual coupon where I/2 = semiannual interest payment
M = par value
k_d = required rate of return on debt or YTM (divide by 2 to adjust for semiannual interest payment)
n = # years to maturity

Source: Brigham & Gapenski 1990, 97.

Alternatively, knowing the current market price of the bond allows the investor to solve for k_d, the yield-to-maturity. It is clear from the formula that the higher the interest rate at which future returns are discounted, the lower will be the present value of that income and vice versa. In short, the equation demonstrates the fact that bond prices vary inversely with the market rate of interest.

The formula also shows that the market prices of longer term instruments will fluctuate more widely for a given change in k_d or YTM than prices of shorter term debt instruments since instruments with a longer term to maturity contain larger powers in the formula. This is important because it means that longer bonds are more subject to capital gains and losses than shorter bonds (Havrilesky 1982, 141).

Although not directly linked to the concept of yield-to-maturity, total returns on fixed-income securities are generated in part due to yield movements. Total return can be defined as the coupon income plus reinvestment of the income plus any change in the market value of a bond over a certain period (First Boston 1981, 50). Since bond prices and yields move in opposite directions, rising interest rates and yields give rise to falling bond prices which in turn hinder total return performance. An examination of Table 7 shows the erratic and volatile nature of calendar-year U.S. government note and bond total returns. Using the period 1975-85 for illustration purposes, annual returns varied over a range of (4.0) percent to 40.3 percent on long term bonds and 1.4 percent to 29.1 percent on intermediate government securities.

TABLE 7

U.S. GOVERNMENT NOTES & BONDS: TOTAL RETURNS: 1975-1985 (IN PERCENT)		
CALENDAR YEAR	LONG TERM GOVERNMENT BONDS	INTERMEDIATE TERM GOVERNMENT NOTES
1975	9.2	7.8
1976	16.8	12.9
1977	(0.7)	1.4
1978	(1.2)	3.5
1979	(1.2)	4.1
1980	(4.0)	3.9
1981	1.8	9.5
1982	40.3	29.1
1983	0.7	7.4
1984	15.4	14.0
1985	31.0	20.3

Source: Ibbotson 1989, 172-179.

This volatility is reemphasized by examining Table 8 where the annualized monthly standard deviations of returns for these same categories are displayed. Variability, using this measure, increased nearly *fivefold* for long term government bonds between 1978 and 1980 and nearly *eightfold* for intermediate government securities.

TABLE 8

U. S. GOVERNMENT NOTES & BONDS ANNUALIZED MONTHLY STANDARD DEVIATIONS OF RETURNS BY YEAR (IN PERCENT)		
CALENDAR YEAR	LONG TERM GOVERNMENT BONDS	INTERMEDIATE TERM GOVERNMENT NOTES
1975	8.38	5.29
1976	4.71	3.80
1977	5.55	2.70
1978	4.49	2.01
1979	10.90	7.02
1980	21.33	15.93
1981	22.16	10.82
1982	10.51	7.03
1983	11.33	5.35
1984	11.54	6.35
1985	12.22	5.64

Source: Ibbotson 1989, 103.

Similar results were discovered relative to U.S. Treasury *bill* variability and risk in a study conducted by Michael Cox in 1984 (Cox 1984, 227).

Upon examination of the above information and data, many questions are raised. The focus of this study addresses one of these key questions. Specifically, given the extreme yield movements and variability in annual rates of return on the Treasury securities noted in the data presented above, is it possible for investors to predict these market movements accurately in advance of their occurrence by using the information contained in the auction results of U.S. Treasury securities?

By means of empirical testing following a complete review of the pertinent literature, this study is designed to answer this fundamental question.

HISTORY AND BACKGROUND

Portfolio Management Techniques

By the time we entered the decade of the 1980s much psychological damage had already been done to the financial markets, it's investors and the general public. Some economists began quoting the "misery index," which was defined as the sum total of inflation and unemployment. During 1980 this index peaked at 20.5 percent, reaching it's highest level since the Great Depression (Streifford 1990, 11).

Long term government and corporate bond investors had just experienced several consecutive years of *negative total returns* (See Table 6). Even these results do not fully reflect the adversity of the situation since they do not incorporate the loss of purchasing power that is experienced by the fixed-income investor due to inflation. Given this scenario, most fixed-income investors were interested in considering any methods which might aid in protecting their portfolios from further erosion of principal. In response, a host of different portfolio management and trading techniques gained popularity and credibility.

Dedication of portfolios became a popular technique to fund a given liability stream. Using this approach, each liability was directly and specifically matched with cash flows from the asset portfolio (Fabozzi, 1990, 47). It was also known as the "cash matching" approach and was considered a desirable portfolio alternative since it did not require the portfolio to be rebalanced during the funding period.

Immunization strategies also became popular during this era. Classic immunization can be defined as a specialized technique for constructing and rebalancing a bond portfolio in order to achieve a target return over a specific investment horizon (Langetieg 1990, 36). Active portfolio management is suspended other than for rebalancing purposes. Bierwag found that perfect immunization can be attained only through the use of default-free zero-coupon bonds which match the planning horizon exactly (Bierwag 1987, 204). This result occurs because only with a zero-coupon bond does the "duration" of the security equal its maturity. Duration is a more accurate measure of bond price volatility because it considers not only the final payment received at maturity but all interim cash flows as well (Kaufman 1989, 97, 338).

Contingent immunization techniques also gained popularity during this period. Contingent immunization allows for active management of the portfolio as long as portfolio return exceeds a "safety net return." If the return on the portfolio falls to the safety-net level, the portfolio is immunized and active management is halted. The manager can therefore continue to pursue an active strategy until an adverse investment experience (typically a surge in interest rates) drives the available combined return (from active and immunized strategy) down to the safety-net level. Should that happen, the manager is then obliged to immunize the entire portfolio and lock in the safety-net return (Fong 1990, 52).

The use of interest rate futures expanded rapidly throughout this period as well. A futures contract can be defined as a forward contract in which the terms are standardized. The contract is traded on an organized exchange and follows a daily settlement procedure in which the losses of one party are paid to the other party (Chance 1989, 247). Introduction of the first financial futures contracts occurred in 1975 on Government National Mortgage Association (GNMA) securities. This was soon followed by a 90 day Treasury bill contract in 1976 and a Treasury bond contract in 1977 (Chance, 250). These contracts gave the fixed income investor the opportunity to offset or "hedge" risks incurred in the cash market by taking opposite positions in the futures market. By 1986 Chance estimated that financial futures trading was nearly double its closest competitor contract, which was energy at that time. In related research done by Barro, a strong case is made for creating a futures contract using the inflation indices. He contends that price quotes on futures contracts would give investors information they currently do not have on future inflationary expectations and thus reduce the variability of other related macroeconomic variables (Barro 1986, S34).

Interest rate swaps achieved ever-increasing popularity during the early 1980s. An interest rate swap is a financial transaction in which fixed interest is exchanged for floating interest of the same currency. The key principle underlying all swaps is one participant exchanging an advantage in one credit market for an advantage available to another participant in a different credit market. The swap market had grown from nonexistence in 1981 to 170 billion dollars by year end 1985 (Whittaker 1990, 73-77).

"Riding the yield curve" was another portfolio investment tactic which gained increasing acceptance during this period. This technique involves buying slightly longer term securities than the expected holding period during periods of positive yield curves and selling them prior to maturity. Grieves found that this portfolio technique worked exceedingly well during the years 1949-88 (Grieves 1990, 89).

Many fixed income investors, although relieved to have the additional tools mentioned above at their disposal, were interested in approaching portfolio management more actively and aggressively. Many of these investors undertook "rate anticipation swaps" wherein the portfolio manager anticipates an important change in the level or structure of interest rates. For example, if the manager expected interest rates to rise, rate anticipation swaps designed to shorten average portfolio duration would be undertaken (Homer 1972, 92). Given the excessive variability in rates mentioned earlier, this technique was very productive and rewarding when *accurate* forecasts were available but proved disastrous when forecasts went astray.

The following sections address the question of yield curve theory and interest rate forecasts and whether it is reasonable to assume that consistently accurate forecasts can be produced.

Classical Yield Curve Theories

Before addressing the specific question of forecasting *future* rates of interest, it is necessary that the reader be familiar with four basic theories which have evolved as attempts to explain the *present* shape of the yield curve and it's relationship to future rates of interest.

The *expectations theory* of the term structure of yield essentially contends that the present yield curve reflects a perfect prediction of future yields. The unbiased expectations theory asserts that expected future interest rates are equal to forward rates computed from observed bond prices (Weston & Copeland 1986, 146). Thus, an upward sloping yield curve is predictive of higher yields in the future. Conversely a negative or downward sloping yield curve predicts lower yields in the future. Many researchers have tested this theory with mixed results.

Campbell's work reaffirmed the validity of the expectations hypothesis (Campbell, 1986, 183). On the other hand, both Mankiw (1986, 63) and Pesando (1988, 238) found evidence which contradicts the expectations hypothesis. Elliott (1976, 40) found modest evidence to support the expectations theory in the short end of the yield curve with securities less than eight years to maturity. Fama (1990, 59) found that the term structure shows little power to forecast near term changes in the one year interest rate. Finally, later work by Campbell (1989, 77) somewhat reversed his earlier findings, since he found expectations effects *only* in the short end of the yield curve. On balance, evidence for the validity of the expectations hypothesis is weak.

The *market segmentation theory* states that each lender and borrower has a preferred maturity range. This theory contends that the slope of the yield curve depends on the supply and demand conditions that exist in the long term and short term areas of the market (Brigham 1989, 87). For example, banks may have a tendency to operate in the Treasury bill market while pension funds are active in the 20-30 year market. If an accurate analysis of the supply and demand for funds is undertaken in each of these market "segments," relative pressures can be ascertained and judgements can be made regarding the future course of the term structure. A study done by Christofides (1980, 114) using Canadian data strongly supported the use of the market segmentation approach as helpful in determining the term structure of interest rates. On the other hand, Elliott in a study covering U.S. Treasury securities over the 1964-1972 period, found evidence of yield curve "segments" in the maturity ranges beyond seven years *only* (Elliott 1976, 46).

The *liquidity preference theory* attempts to explain why the yield curve has a positive term premium. The term premium is the difference between a long term U.S. government bond's yield and the yield on a one month Treasury bill (Kiem 1986, 371). According to the liquidity preference theory, this difference is positive because investors prefer to lend money short and borrowers prefer to borrow long. Due to this pressure imbalance, the "normal" shape of the yield curve is upward sloping (Brigham & Gapenski 1988, 75).

The last theory used to explain the term structure of rates is known as the *preferred habitat theory* (Modigliani 1966, 183). This particular theory draws upon the other three theories and states that the spread between long and short rates should depend primarily on the expected change in the long rate. It suggests that the spread is also influenced by supply and demand considerations as well.

As mentioned earlier, each of these term structure theories offer some assistance in forecasting future rates of interest. Unfortunately, no *single* concept has proven itself infallible under *all* circumstances.

Yield Curve Theory - Other Factors

Since the four theories mentioned previously provide no firm decision rules for forecasting interest rates, a deeper examination of other key influencing factors is warranted.

According to Michael Parkin, two other variables *influence the level of interest rates. He has identified these as monetary and fiscal policy.* Parkin explains that changes in the money supply (monetary policy) affect aggregate demand by changing interest rates. Furthermore, changes in government purchases or tax policy (fiscal policy) affect not only real GNP but interest rates as well. Therefore, these two factors require additional exploration (Parkin 1990, 768).

The first variable, monetary policy, is established by the Federal Open Market Committee (FOMC). This arm of the Federal Reserve holds meetings eight times a year in Washington D.C. for the purpose of determining what transactions the Federal Reserve will conduct in the open market (Board of Governors of the Federal Reserve System 1985, 6). These open market operations are carried out under the general direction of the FOMC and are the most powerful and flexible monetary policy tool of the Federal Reserve. They determine the amount of nonborrowed reserves available to the depository system (Byrns Macroeconomics 1989, 240).

The most common of the open market operations is a repurchase agreement. A repurchase agreement involves an agreement between the Open Market Trading Desk and securities dealers to buy securities from dealers, subject to dealer repurchase at the end of a specified period, sometimes as short as one day. Similarly, a matched sales agreement is accomplished by the sale of securities to dealers concurrent with a Federal Reserve agreement to buy them back at the end of the agreed upon period (Cooper 1987, 110). The former action provides reserves to depository institutions and the latter action absorbs reserves. Both of these activities are scrutinized very carefully by the investment community as they seek clues on the future course of monetary policy.

The reason for this concern is the belief that changes in monetary policy, with unpredictable lags, will influence inflation, economic activity, interest rates and thus bond prices. Research done by Robinson in 1984 showed that monetary policy is effective in influencing inflation *only* when combined with credible fiscal policies (Robinson 1984, 47). Judging from the data shown earlier in Tables 3 and 4, it is apparent that fiscal credibility was lacking during the time frame under study.

One monetary "experiment" that took place during the early 1980s deserves special mention. In October 1979, the Federal Reserve under the leadership of Paul Volcker announced a dramatic and substantive change in monetary policy (Pesando 1988, 217). With annualized inflation rates reaching nearly 20 percent, it was decided that stern action could wait no longer (Cargill 1991, 281). Before the change, monetary policy had been conducted by targeting short-term interest rates. The new policy involved targeting monetary aggregates and was followed shortly thereafter by a redefinition of those aggregates. These changes coupled with other changing market dynamics gave rise to a marked increase in the level *and* volatility of interest rates in both Canada (Pesando 1988, 217) and the United States (Walsh 1984, 133). Marsh (1983, 644) also found "period specific" fluctuations in other macroeconomic variables such as industrial production during this same period.

This experiment proved to be relatively short-lived as it was abandoned in 1982. Fair determined that aside from this three year interval, the Federal Reserve has targeted interest rates in conducting monetary policy. Furthermore, he found that the use of interest rate targeting is a superior policy instrument under most conditions (Fair 1988, 301).

Kahn (1990, 61) found that changes in interest rates on real output are less pronounced, take longer to be realized and are more uncertain than in the past. In confirming the Kahn study, Benjamin Friedman (1990, 77) found that major changes in the U.S. economy over the past 25 years had made monetary policy a less reliable policy tool than in years prior. Roberds (1990, 64) found that the short-term predictive usefulness of the monetary aggregates has greatly diminished during the 1980s due largely to the changing composition of the monetary aggregates during that time. Screpanti (1989, 188) found that monetary policy *alone* would not be successful in influencing the interest rate primarily because of the interactions of speculators who are unwilling or unable to forecast the long term effects of fundamental changes in monetary policy. Meltzer (1984, 446) determined that the adoption of a monetary growth "rule" (ala Milton Friedman) coupled with a *proper, specified, enforceable* fiscal policy would lead eventually to lower interest rates and reduce uncertainty.

As noted above, the literature on the Federal Reserve conduct of monetary policy is not encouraging with respect to interest rate forecasting. Since monetary policy dynamics contributed to the general level of volatility and uncertainty in the early 1980s, it offers few additional tools for use in interest rate forecasting.

The second variable identified by Parkin was government *fiscal policy*. According to Weston and Brigham (1990, 97), the necessity of funding large government deficits "crowds out" other borrowers and places upward pressure on interest rates. The actual research on "crowding out" theory is far from conclusive. For example, Swamy (1990, 1026) found some modest linkage between federal deficits and short-term interest rates using regression analysis with a one quarter lag. Both Hoelscher (1986, 1) and Thomas (1988, 150) found evidence of a strong linkage between deficits and long term interest rates. Cebula (1981, 335) found clear evidence that private investment was crowded out by government spending. Wachtel (1987, 1012) found that unexpected increases in the size of deficit projections made by the Congressional Budget Office or the Office of Management of the Budget had produced an immediate impact on long term government bond yields. Both Herman (1987, 32) and Gilpin (1990, 12) noted that as Congress worked toward a credible plan to reduce deficits, interest rates declined indicating a confirmation of crowding out effects from a reverse perspective.

However, Evans (1985, 68), Darrat (1990, 752), Webster (1983, 587) and Schirm (1989, 400) all found little or no support for the traditional crowding out theory. Bowles (1989, 203) found the results highly subject to the methodology and time period used. A study by McCallum (1984, 123) addressed the question of bond financed deficits but only insofar as their ultimate impact on the price level.

Since research on fiscal policy and the "crowding out" theory is so varied it is difficult to draw any conclusions on the subject. Because of this situation, the direct study of fiscal policy and government deficits is of limited value in determining the future direction of interest rates.

Forecasting - An Overview

The key overriding question which has yet to be addressed is: "Can interest rates be forecasted with accuracy?" According to Fischer (1991, 346), an interest rate forecasting model must encompass four inter-related steps including: 1) the assumption of a broad economic model, 2) forecasts of business activity, 3) integration of a supply and demand for funds forecast and 4) the overlay of expected monetary and fiscal policy.

Regardless of the specific model used, the research indicates interest rate forecasting is fraught with error. For example, Pesando's 1988 study on the accuracy of Canadian interest rate predictions found that the "experts" forecasts over the study period were actually less accurate than a naive "no change" prediction (Pesando 1988, 238). Pesando's earlier 1981 study found that forecasters successfully forecast near term movements in short-term rates but could not forecast near term movements in long-term rates (Pesando 1981, 305).

Fraser (1977, 38) performed a study on U.S. interest rates covering the 1974-76 period and found a similar record of poor forecasting performance. He found very large forecast errors in both short and long-term rates and also found a naive "no change" prediction had outperformed the "experts." Prell, using the 1969-1972 period, also found forecasts by 23 market "professionals" to have large forecast errors on all seven different rates which he studied. Even more interesting, he found substantial errors in forecasting the *direction* of rates (Prell 1973, 5).

The forecasting record described above is less than stellar. Nonetheless, the quest for the ultimate forecasting tool continues. Whether it be sun spots, put-call ratios, or moving averages, market participants continue to search for accurate forecasting methodologies. Even in 1935, John Maynard Keynes made the following observation regarding forecasting in his classic work *The Theory of Employment, Interest and Money*:

> But there is one feature in particular which deserves our attention. It might have been supposed that competition between expert professionals, possessing judgement and knowledge beyond that of the average private investor, would correct the vagaries of the ignorant individual left to himself. It happens however, that the energies and skill of the professional investor and speculator are mainly occupied otherwise. For most of those persons are in fact largely concerned, not with making superior long-term forecasts of the probable yield of an investment over its whole life, but with foreseeing changes in the conventional basis of valuation a short time ahead of the general public. They are concerned, not with what an investment is really worth to a man who buys it "for keeps" but with what the market will value it at, under the influence of mass psychology, three months or a year hence. Moreover, this behavior is not the outcome of wrong-headed propensity. It is an inevitable result of an investment market organized along the lines described. For it is not sensible to pay 25 for an investment of which you believe the prospective yield to justify a value of 30, if you believe that the market will value it at 20 three months hence.
>
> Thus the professional investor is forced to concern himself with the anticipation of impending changes, in the news or in the atmosphere, of the kind by which

experience shows that the mass psychology of the market is most influenced (Keynes 1935, 154-155).

As noted above, forecasting has been an obsession with market professionals for some time. Distinctions made between the 1930s and 1980s are only a matter of degree, not of kind. In the 1930s, Keynes speaks of investors who make investment and trading decisions based upon three month time horizons. In the volatile 1980s environment many sophisticated professional investors, in an attempt to outperform the competition, have found it necessary to compress these time horizons from years and months to hours and minutes.

Treasury Auction Procedures - An Overview

Given the intense pressure to perform, fixed-income market participants continue to look for signals they can use as forecasting tools. Many actual market participants scrutinize the auction results of U.S. Treasury debt instruments because they believe these results offer some clue to future near-term market movements. Schirm (1989, 394) found that U.S. government primary dealers employ their own Treasury debt forecasters which indicates that they place a high value on future Treasury financing activities. Calvo (1988, 659) found that expectations play a crucial role in the auction of government debt to the public when interest rates are not pegged. Pegging of rates ended on March 4, 1951 with the signing of the Treasury-Federal Reserve Accord, thus ending the nine year experience with pegged interest rates (Miller 1985, 575).

In order to ascertain the usefulness of Treasury auction results in forecasting future rates of interest, a detailed explanation of the intricacies of U.S. Treasury auction methods is necessary. This explanation includes a discussion of several related issues including: 1) the role of "non-competitive" bids in the auction process, 2) current controversial "competitive" bidding procedures, 3) evidence of collusion in bidding on the part of primary dealers, 4) proposed new bidding procedures, and 5) specific previous research which tends to confirm or refute the original hypothesis.

Treasury securities are fixed-income instruments which are issued by and carry the full faith and credit guarantee of the U.S.

government. They are issued in varying maturities ranging from three months to 30 years and sizes as small as $1000. On a well publicized schedule, the Treasury announces and then sells to the public bills, notes and bonds. The specific maturities presently offered on a regular basis are as follows:

> 3 month bills
> 6 month bills
> 1 year bills
> 2 year notes
> 3 year notes
> 4 year notes
> 5 year notes
> 7 year notes
> 10 year notes
> 30 year bonds

Although different nomenclature is used to describe these securities, they are all guaranteed by the U.S. government. The reason for the distinction is simply based on the original maturity of the instrument. Additionally, the auction methods and rules used to sell these securities are ordinarily the same (First Boston 1990, 61).

These securities can be purchased by the public using either one of two bidding methods. The typical small individual investor places a "non-competitive" bid (Gitman & Joehnk 1990, 155). This option allows the small investor to purchase the Treasury security directly from the Treasury without incurring any brokerage charges (Brennan 1989, 74). The non-competitive bids are filled by the Treasury at the quantity-weighted average of all accepted competitive bids. Thus they perform a role similar to a "buy at market" order which is used in the equity markets (Smith 1966, 142). These orders, by definition, do not state a price or yield only a dollar amount and therefore benefit small, infrequent buyers since they are assured of buying the amount of desired securities at the *average* auction price (Sivesind 1978, 34). In his research Sivesind also pointed out that although the number of non-competitive bids far outweighed the number of competitive bids, the vast *dollar amount* of bids come from competitive bidders (Sivesend 1987, 35).

The current "competitive" bidding procedures are used by large financial institutions and, most importantly, "primary dealers." Primary dealers consist of an elite core of approximately 38 Wall Street investment banking concerns and money center banks. The Federal Reserve Bank of New York confers (or revokes) the primary dealer status of these firms (Siconolfi 1991, A5). These dealers are expected to maintain a certain level of capital, actively maintain secondary markets in U.S. Treasury securities and, most importantly, bid on the Treasury sale of new debt securities. In return for these commitments, the Treasury gives certain benefits to these 38 dealers, such as opportunities to comment upon and review upcoming debt issuance plans.

The primary dealers typically bid on a "competitive" basis when bidding for new Treasury securities since non-competitive bids are limited to a maximum of 5 million dollars per investor (Thomas October 28,1991, pp.C1, C16). This method, known technically as a "discriminatory auction," means that the Treasury sells securities to different bidders at different prices (Bolten 1973, 577) and that each successful bidder pays the actual price bid rather than a single price common to all bidders (Harris 1981, 1477). In fact, each competitive bidder may submit as many bids as they desire provided the bidder does not purchase more than 35 percent of the entire issue. The Treasury satisfies all non-competitive bids first and then fills the remainder of the offering from the competitive tenders proceeding from the highest to the lowest accepted price until the issue is fully subscribed. Tenders submitted below the lowest accepted price, known as the stop-out price, are not filled (Sivesind 1978, 34). Those bids which are precisely at the stop-out price are awarded a percentage of the quantity requested.

Research by Scott in 1979 shows that securities dealers optimize their bidding results via the use of multiple price bids or "strip bids" in the U.S. Treasury Bill market (Scott 1979, 280). Later work by Boatler confirmed that dealers do actually submit "scale-out" bids as an offer to purchase Treasury Bills if bargain prices become available (Boatler 1985, 38). Wachtel discovered in his 1990 work that this procedure is also prevalent in the bidding on Treasury notes and bonds (Wachtel 1990, 64).

This type of auction method is a mixed blessing for primary dealers. First, the timely submission of the bids is critical. As one large primary dealer discovered on January third, 1985, a bid which was submitted to the New York Federal Reserve Bank seconds after the 1 P.M. New York deadline was rejected (Marcial 1985, 76). Competing dealers assumed that the dealer was forced to cover for the error in the secondary market, most likely at a loss. Second, the dealer must very carefully determine what price to bid for the security. The objective is to buy the securities at the lowest or cut-off or stop-out price. If the dealer bids too low the securities may be missed entirely and higher prices may have to be paid in the secondary market. Conversely, if the dealer bids too high, they may own overpriced securities which can only be sold at a loss (Wallace 1985, 96). This latter concern is sometimes dubbed the "winners curse" and is defined as the dubious distinction of the award of an object because the winning party most *overestimated* it's value. (Engelbrecht-Wiggans 1980, 133).

Because of the bidding procedure described above, some well known economists and other "market watchers" contend that this auction structure and process is conducive to collusion. The primary dealer network does possess the characteristics which are typically associated with a "pure" oligopolistic market structure where a tendency to collude in many cases does exist (Byrns Microeconomics 1989, 224). These characteristics include: 1) economies of scale which lead to a small number of dominant firms, 2) substantial barriers to entry, 3) non-price competition, 4) recognized mutual interdependence, 5) incentive to merge and 6) *temptation to collude* (Waud 1989, 272).

With enormous capital and commensurately large trading desks, the primary dealers certainly possess large economies of scale. Since the U.S. Treasury confers a total of only 38-40 primary dealerships, the acquisition of primary dealer status is a substantial barrier to entry as many large institutional clients will only transact business with primary dealers. The Treasury market is believed to be very efficient, particularly in the short maturity area with only minuscule price disparities between dealers. This fact forces dealers to compete on grounds other than price. As discussed by Scott, dealers openly exchange views about the market among themselves as well as other institutional investors until immediately before auction time, thus confirming the interdependence of decision making (Scott 1979, 280). There has also been evidence of merger activity among firms, but the most critical characteristic mentioned above involves the issue of collusion.

Simply because an industry has some characteristics of oligopoly, in no way proves collusion. Michael Rieber concluded that actual collusion is highly unlikely in the Treasury Bill market between securities dealers (Reiber 1965, 49). Conversely, Boatler found possible evidence of collusion in his study covering Treasury Bill bids between 1952-1959 (Boatler 1985, 39). Milton Friedman's research done in 1963 finds a strong incentive for collusion in current bidding practices but *no actual evidence* of it (Friedman 1991, A10). Given the mixed evidence available, it seems premature to conclude that collusion is practiced, although recent market events suggest it is a possibility.

These recent events include the admission by Salomon Brothers, a very large primary dealer, that they controlled an astonishing 94 percent of the two-year Treasury notes which were sold at auction in May of 1991 (Cohen September 5, 1991, pp. C1,C6). This obviously violates the previously mentioned Treasury rule which states that no single bidder may purchase more than 35 percent of any single issue being sold (Cohen August 21 1991, C1). This admission has sparked inquiries by Congress and the SEC about how pervasive this type of activity has been. The SEC probe is seeking information back to January of 1990 which specifically relates to "sharing, swapping or exchange of information" about U.S. Treasury securities auctions. The agency wants to know about "actual or proposed agreements, arrangements or understandings" relating to any such information sharing (Cohen August 27,1991, C1). The U.S. Treasury has studied all of it's note and bond auctions since 1986, a total of more than two hundred, and has found *little evidence* of collusion except for the recent Salomon incident (Cohen August 21, 1991, C1).

Even without present clear-cut evidence of collusion, there exists a contingent of economists and other financial experts who contend that the temptation to collude under the present system is simply too great, and the bidding procedure should be changed. Most researchers who have studied the issue agree that the present system should be replaced with a "competitive" auction. The terminology is confusing because that is what current market participants and the

Treasury call the present system, when it can more accurately be described a "discriminatory" procedure as discussed above.

Confusing terminology aside, a competitive auction bidding system would clear the market supply at *one* price where the demand equalled the supply. Bidders below the clearing price would be forced out of the market (unsatisfied) and bidders above the clearing price would have their demand satisfied at a price lower than they were willing to pay (Bolten 1973, 578). This would of course eliminate the possibility of the "winners curse" described above since all purchasers would buy at the same price.

Research done on this topic points to an additional major advantage. Work done by Harris (1981, 1479), Smith (1966, 141), Bolten (1973, 584) and Friedman (1963, 318) all indicate that conversion to a competitive auction would yield *more* revenue to the U.S. Treasury through the receipt of lower average yields and higher average prices on the securities sold.

Although such dramatic changes may not be forthcoming immediately, less dramatic steps are already being undertaken by the Treasury in an attempt to forestall criticism (Salwen September 9,1991, C1). The most critical new requirement makes it mandatory for customers who buy large amounts of Treasury securities at auction through dealers to verify their purchase *in writing* before accepting delivery (Wessel, September 12, 1991, C1). This would presumably eliminate the problem of dealers bidding for customers without their knowledge or authorization.

Because of the controversy mentioned above, attention to the use of U.S. Treasury auction results as an interest rate forecasting tool may have been diverted. The literature available on this subject is quite limited but very instructive. In a study of U.S. Treasury *Bill* auctions, Cammack (1987, 2) found a tendency for yields in the secondary Bill market to rise (prices fall) when the auction results revealed a dispersion of opinion on the value of the security or "Tail" larger than expected. She also discovered that secondary Treasury bill prices increased when the number of bidders or the "Coverage Ratio" was larger than expected. In a study of all Treasury auctions from October 1979 through March 1985, Wachtel discovered that indicators of demand strength and uncertainty are positively and significantly related to yield changes on the auction day (Wachtel, 1990, 70).

These studies are extremely important as they confirm what fixed-income market participants had surmised for some time. The other recent revelations previously mentioned regarding a major securities dealer's alleged improprieties when bidding on U.S. Treasury issues also suggests that this information is of value to market participants.

Given this confluence of recent and past events, a study which focuses on the use of Treasury auction results as interest rate predictors is deemed warranted.

METHODOLOGY

Population and Sampling Techniques

In order to determine if Treasury *note or bond auction* results do in fact provide information useful in the prediction of future interest rate movements, several decisions were required. The first decision related to the historical context of the study.

During the decade of the 1980s, U.S. Treasury financing needs and securities sales grew at an extremely rapid pace with the combination of the Reagan supply-side tax cuts and simultaneous defense build-up (See Table 4). In addition to the Reagan initiatives of the 1980s, previous problems inherited from the 1970s compounded the situation and put the economy, inflation and interest rates on a roller coaster throughout the decade. For example, interest rates, as measured by the three-month Treasury bill rate, ranged from a low of five percent to a high of 17 percent. Annual rates of change in real GNP varied from negative 2.5 percent during the 1982 recession, to a positive rate of 6.8 percent in 1984, only two short years later. Finally, inflation which was rising at an annual rate of approximately 14 percent at the beginning of the decade, dropped to an annual rate of gain of 2 percent by 1986 and ended the decade at approximately a 4 percent rate of increase (Bronfenbrenner, 1990, 2).

Given the incredible volatility noted above, a decade long study encompassing the 1980-1989 time period seemed certain to pass any test for rigor and diversity.

The second decision involved the question of which *specific* Treasury notes or bonds to include in the study. As of early 1990, the U.S. Treasury auctioned a two-year note on a monthly basis and three, four, five, seven and ten-year notes on a quarterly basis. In addition, the Treasury auctioned a thirty-year bond on a quarterly cycle. Since the *thirty-year bond* is the only bond which the Treasury auctions, it clearly *must* be included in the study.

As to the question of an appropriate note to study, the previously mentioned research indicated there were six different notes from which to choose. Wachtel's 1990 research determined that there was very little disparity in results among the various auctions used in that study (Wachtel 1990, 69). Given this information, a decision to study the *five-year note* was reached for the following reasons:

1) The thirty-year bond was issued quarterly (at that time). Therefore, for maximum compatibility with other data, it seemed advisable to choose a note issue which was also issued quarterly. This eliminated the two-year note as it was sold on a monthly basis. (Note: The five-year note was shifted to a monthly issue in January of 1990, but during the decade of this study, the issue was sold quarterly).

2) The three and ten-year note, although sold quarterly, were sold on consecutive days preceding the thirty-year bond. Distortion effects from these logistics seemed quite probable; therefore, the three and ten-year note were eliminated from consideration.

3) This reduced the potential study candidates to the four, five or seven-year note. As will be explained in more detail, the four-year note was dropped from consideration since some necessary data were unavailable. The remaining two issues were sold in isolation during different times of the quarter thus eliminating the potential for distortion. Since the five-year note resides at the mid-point of the ten-year note range, the five year note was chosen for the study.

This is the rationale for choosing the *five-year note* and the *thirty-year bond* as the focus of this study.

By using this carefully selected data sample and ten-year historical perspective, the results obtained from this study can legitimately be applied to the broader population of all Treasury note and bond auctions.

Presentation of Data

The next methodological issue to be addressed was the question of what data should be used in the study. All auction results include several critical pieces of data which are worthy of analysis and displayed on the following pages in Tables 9 and 10. Table 9 displays all independent variables related to the five-year auctions in the study and Table 10 displays the independent variables related to the thirty-year auctions. The following explanation of the independent variables relates to both tables.

Column (1) displays the exact date upon which the auction took place. Column (2) displays the final coupon rate which was assigned to the security upon completion of the auction. Column (3) displays the total dollar amount of actual bids or "tenders" received on the issue being sold, expressed in millions of dollars. Column (4) indicates the actual amount of the issue being auctioned, again expressed in millions of dollars.

Column (5) is a calculated field entitled "Coverage Ratio." This column is calculated by dividing column (3) by column (4). Column (6) displays the highest percentage yield at which the Treasury accepted bids for the issue. As previously explained, the Treasury first satisfies all non-competitive bids at the quantity-weighted average of all accepted bids. This produces the "Average Yield" displayed, in percentage, in Column (7). Once the average yield has been established, the Treasury then assigns a coupon rate which is typically the next one-eighth percent increment above the average yield. This produces a slightly discounted price on the newly-issued security for those investors who purchased at the average yield. The Treasury then begins awarding bids to competitive bidders starting with the highest price (lowest yield) and then proceeding to lower prices (higher yields) until the issue has been fully subscribed. The highest yield (lowest price) at which the securities are sold is shown in Column (6). At this highest awarded yield (or stop-out price) the Treasury only accepts enough tenders to complete the sale of the issue. Therefore, in most cases the investor bidding at the high yield only receives a portion of the amount for which they bid. This percentage is displayed in Column (8) and is titled "Percent Accepted at the High Yield."

TABLE 9

FIVE YEAR AUCTION RESULTS

DATE of AUCTION (1)	COUPON RATE (2)	TOTAL TENDERS (3)	TOTAL SOLD (4)	CVRGE RATIO (5) **	HIGH YIELD (6)	AVERAGE YIELD (7)	%ACCPT H YLD (8)
22680	14.375	4824	2500	1.93	14.50	14.39	45
60380	9.625	5650	3004	1.88	9.69	9.66	60
82780	11.750	7433	3001	2.48	11.78	11.76	40
120380	13.500	7509	3004	2.50	13.54	13.52	93
22681	13.750	7939	3254	2.44	13.81	13.79	44
52881	13.875	4999	3000	1.67	14.02	13.95	81
82781	16.125	6462	3251	1.99	16.19	16.14	16
112481	12.750	8252	3254	2.54	12.85	12.83	25
22482	14.000	6481	3251	1.99	14.05	14.01	16
52582	13.750	9643	3758	2.57	13.73	13.71	41
83182	12.625	11078	4762	2.33	12.69	12.68	88
112382	10.125	10184	5004	2.04	10.23	10.21	18
22383	9.875	10944	5500	1.99	10.00	9.96	15
60183	10.500	12980	5763	2.25	10.50	10.50	97
83183	11.750	12173	6003	2.03	11.82	11.79	1
112983	11.375	17866	6013	2.97	11.37	11.37	80
22884	11.750	14065	6024	2.33	11.85	11.84	39
53184	13.875	14726	6251	2.36	13.96	13.93	75
82984	12.750	16738	6530	2.56	12.78	12.78	96
112884	11.000	18977	6757	2.81	11.03	11.02	63
22685	11.375	19252	7005	2.75	11.43	11.43	80
52985	9.875	15196	7012	2.17	9.96	9.95	67
82885	9.625	23389	7254	3.22	9.63	9.62	16
112785	9.125	25110	7519	3.34	9.13	9.13	60
22686	8.125	19156	7520	2.55	8.13	8.12	43
52886	7.500	18080	7756	2.33	7.55	7.53	65
82786	6.500	22588	8017	2.82	6.52	6.51	41
112586	6.625	25025	8286	3.02	6.67	6.66	67
22587	6.625	26757	8261	3.24	6.74	6.73	42
52787	8.250	23556	8075	2.92	8.27	8.27	95
82887	8.375	19116	7762	2.46	8.49	8.48	70
112487	8.250	20149	7505	2.68	8.31	8.30	65
22588	7.625	22067	7252	3.04	7.66	7.65	78
52688	8.750	24499	7001	3.50	8.77	8.77	65
82488	9.000	21568	7268	2.97	9.04	9.04	82
112388	8.875	21793	7504	2.90	8.98	8.97	3
22389	9.500	21739	7812	2.78	9.49	9.49	71
52589	8.625	20752	7507	2.76	8.72	8.72	98
82389	8.250	26150	7800	3.35	8.26	8.26	60
112989	7.750	23585	8045	2.93	7.78	7.77	39

** Indicates calculated field

Source: Department of the U.S. Treasury, 1980-89, Various News Releases.

TABLE 9 (CONTINUED)

FIVE YEAR AUCTION RESULTS

DATE of AUCTION (1)	TAIL (9)	NCOMP BIDS (10)	NCOMPS as % TOTL (11)	NYFD ACC BIDS (12)	NYFDACC as % TOTL (13)	NYFD APPL (14)	NYFDACC as%APPL (15)
	**		**		**		**
22680	11	253	10.1				
60380	3	336	11.2				
82780	2	441	14.7				
120380	2	512	17.0	2418	80.5	6365	38.0
22681	2	448	13.8	2751	84.6	6833	40.3
52881	7	517	17.2	2153	71.8	3847	56.0
82781	5	490	15.1	2614	80.4	5335	49.0
112481	2	574	17.6	2890	88.8	6990	41.3
22482	4	482	14.8	2604	80.1	5164	50.4
52582	2	689	18.3	3169	84.3	7940	39.9
83182	1	1082	22.7	4102	86.1	9196	44.6
112382	2	878	17.5	4501	90.0	8473	53.1
22383	4	911	16.6	4545	82.6	9160	49.6
60183	0	1063	18.4	5037	87.4	10860	46.4
83183	3	1327	22.1	5143	85.7	10215	50.3
112983	0	536	8.9	5576	92.7	15653	35.6
22884	1	482	8.0	5318	88.3	12364	43.0
53184	3	720	11.5	5370	85.9	12851	41.8
82984	0	522	8.0	5984	91.6	14443	41.4
112884	1	479	7.1	6002	88.8	15996	37.5
22685	0	577	8.2	6418	91.6	16647	38.6
52985	1	610	8.7	5764	82.2	12875	44.8
82885	1	638	8.8	6368	87.8	20095	31.7
112785	0	820	10.9	6695	89.0	22445	29.8
22686	1	450	6.0	6533	86.9	16502	39.6
52886	2	337	4.3	7108	91.6	16212	43.8
82786	1	256	3.2	7515	93.7	20163	37.3
112586	1	255	3.1	7833	94.5	22516	34.8
22587	1	266	3.2	6099	73.8	22504	27.1
52787	0	352	4.4	7746	95.9	21405	36.2
82887	1	361	4.7	7248	93.4	17072	42.5
112487	1	291	3.9	6752	90.0	17552	38.5
22588	1	305	4.2	6689	92.2	19764	33.8
52688	0	522	7.5	6555	93.6	22153	29.6
82488	0	600	8.3	6593	90.7	19249	34.3
112388	1	551	7.3	6933	92.4	19308	35.9
22389	0	696	8.9	7144	91.5	19215	37.2
52589	0	562	7.5	6631	88.3	18740	35.4
82389	0	341	4.4	7463	95.7	24112	30.9
112989	1	273	3.4	7719	96.0	21972	35.1

** Indicates calculated field

Source: Department of the U.S. Treasury, 1980-89, Various News Releases.

TABLE 10

THIRTY YEAR AUCTION RESULTS							
DATE of AUCTION (1)	COUPON RATE (2)	TOTAL TENDER (3)	TOTAL SOLD (4)	CVRGE RATIO (5) **	HIGH YIELD (6)	AVERAGE YIELD (7)	% ACCPT H YLD (8)
20780	11.750	4635	2001	2.32	11.87	11.84	62
50880	10.000	3648	2000	1.82	10.18	10.12	55
80780	10.375	2485	1500	1.66	10.80	10.71	46
110780	12.750	3819	2000	1.91	12.87	12.81	47
20581	12.750	5252	2250	2.33	12.70	12.68	84
50781	13.875	5025	2001	2.51	14.01	13.99	89
80681	13.875	4739	2000	2.37	14.08	14.06	88
110581	14.000	3083	2001	1.54	14.24	14.10	12
20482	14.000	5050	2500	2.02	14.61	14.56	19
110982	10.375	7428	3002	2.47	10.48	10.46	70
20383	10.375	6197	3502	1.77	11.05	11.01	56
50583	10.375	7672	3752	2.04	10.32	10.29	76
80483	12.000	8619	4006	2.15	12.10	12.08	94
111083	12.000	9380	4254	2.20	11.82	11.80	37
20984	12.000	11010	4535	2.43	11.88	11.88	87
51084	13.250	10206	4751	2.15	13.34	13.32	68
80984	12.500	16667	4798	3.47	12.52	12.52	57
110884	11.750	9740	5253	1.85	11.87	11.83	14
20785	11.250	12290	5751	2.14	11.31	11.27	13
50985	11.250	15870	6020	2.64	11.39	11.38	36
80885	10.625	15032	6501	2.31	10.68	10.66	91
112285	9.875	14856	6761	2.20	9.95	9.93	22
20686	9.250	17766	7004	2.54	9.29	9.28	47
50886	7.250	19095	9015	2.12	7.40	7.37	21
80786	7.250	17250	9005	1.92	7.65	7.63	58
110686	7.500	21086	9265	2.28	7.56	7.54	42
20587	7.500	26770	9298	2.88	7.50	7.49	49
50787	8.750	20207	9275	2.18	8.77	8.76	92
81387	8.875	30063	9010	3.34	8.89	8.89	91
110587	8.875	20024	4778	4.19	8.79	8.79	76
20488	8.750	17333	8764	1.98	8.53	8.51	81
51288	9.125	21693	8505	2.55	9.18	9.17	74
111788	9.000	21580	9026	2.39	9.11	9.10	37
20989	8.875	17163	9508	1.81	8.95	8.91	12
51189	8.875	20015	9535	2.10	9.12	9.11	51
81089	8.125	20100	9752	2.06	8.15	8.14	53
111489	8.125	20429	10061	2.03	7.87	7.87	97
** Indicates calculated field							

Source: Department of the U.S. Treasury, 1980-89, Various NewsReleases.

TABLE 10 (CONTINUED)

THIRTY YEAR AUCTION RESULTS

DATE of AUCTION (1)	TAIL (9)	NCOMP BIDS (10)	NCOMP as % TOTL (11)	NYFD ACC BIDS (12)	NYFDACC as % TOTL (13)	NYFD APPL (14)	NYFDACC as%APPL (15)
	**		**		**		**
20780	3	204	10.2				
50880	6	182	9.1				
80780	9	116	7.7				
110780	6	142	7.1	1794	89.7	3389	52.9
20581	2	238	10.6	1994	88.6	4617	43.2
50781	2	333	16.6	1744	87.1	4265	40.9
80681	2	448	22.4	1591	79.5	3903	40.8
110581	14	181	9.0	1672	83.6	2524	66.3
20482	5	394	15.8	2123	84.9	4277	49.6
110982	2	701	23.4	2653	88.4	6503	40.8
20383	4	655	18.7	3130	89.4	5445	57.5
50583	3	800	21.3	3259	86.9	6313	51.6
80483	2	984	24.6	3541	88.4	7246	48.9
111083	2	528	12.4	3588	84.3	7602	47.2
20984	0	335	7.4	4252	93.8	10019	42.4
51084	2	371	7.8	4464	94.0	8867	50.4
80984	0	291	6.1	4592	95.7	15068	30.5
110884	4	305	5.8	4805	91.5	8154	58.9
20785	4	375	6.5	5339	92.8	10529	50.7
50985	1	554	9.2	5399	89.7	14173	38.1
80885	2	464	7.1	5996	92.2	13520	44.4
112285	2	340	5.0	6367	94.2	13332	47.8
20686	1	331	4.7	6687	95.5	15678	42.7
50886	3	337	3.7	8553	94.9	17465	49.0
80786	2	195	2.2	8531	94.7	15745	54.2
110686	2	228	2.5	8731	94.2	19409	45.0
20587	1	280	3.0	8796	94.6	24542	35.8
50787	1	362	3.9	8900	96.0	18676	47.7
81387	0	397	4.4	8509	94.4	28077	30.3
110587	0	308	6.4	4539	95.0	18397	24.7
20488	2	327	3.7	8392	95.8	15915	52.7
51288	1	462	5.4	7947	93.4	19838	40.1
111788	1	413	4.6	8594	95.2	20047	42.9
20989	4	307	3.2	9012	94.8	15230	59.2
51189	1	367	3.8	8892	93.3	18353	48.4
81089	1	374	3.8	9274	95.1	18628	49.8
111489	0	342	3.4	9571	95.1	18831	50.8
** Indicates calculated field							

Source: Department of the U.S. Treasury, 1980-89, Various NewsReleases.

The information displayed in Column (9) titled the "Tail" of the issue, is expressed in basis points and is calculated as the difference between Column (6) and Column (7). Column (10) displays the dollar amount of non-competitive, retail-oriented bids received in the auction, expressed in millions. Since auction size has grown dramatically over the period under study, Column (11) displays non-competitive bids as a percentage of the total size of the issue.

Columns (12)-(15) deal with bidding information relating to the New York Federal Reserve district. Beginning in the fourth quarter of 1980, the Treasury began releasing more specific information on the bidding results *from each Federal Reserve district*. Most market participants agree that the activity which occurs in the New York district is largely primary dealer activity since virtually all primary dealers are headquartered in New York City and clear their transactions (including auction purchases) through New York banks. Since this is the case, Column (12) shows the actual dollar amount, in millions, of accepted bids in the New York district. Column (13) is a calculated field indicating the percentage of the total auction which was sold in the New York district. Column (14) indicates the amount of tenders applied for by the New York district, in millions. Finally, Column (15) is a calculated field showing the percentage of New York accepted bids compared to New York applications.

The identification of the dependent variable was the next methodological issue. Given the nature of the research question, the dependent variable must be a U.S. Treasury price or yield change indicator which can be used throughout the period of study. Furthermore, this pricing information on the U.S. government securities must be consistently available before, during and after the auction dates shown in Tables 9 and 10. Since the study centers on five-year and thirty-year securities, secondary market yields on comparable maturity securities should be utilized. This conforms to the approach used by Wachtel in his work referred to earlier (Wachtel 1990, 68).

One key consideration was the question of which secondary market issue should be used as the benchmark. Since the study covered a ten-year period, it was impossible to use a five-year issue because it would mature before the study concluded. Even though a thirty-year issue would not mature, the volatility characteristics of the issue would change considerably as the issue shortened over time.

Thus, using a single issue as a benchmark throughout the study period was not a viable option.

A second possibility was to choose *different* issues as market benchmarks for each succeeding auction. This choice presented two problems. First, continuity from one auction to the next would be lost. Second, in many cases *specific* issues are subject to unusual market action due to peculiarities such as short positions, arbitrages and futures market influences. These peculiarities could significantly affect the market price of the chosen benchmark security and produce results which were not indicative of the broader market.

Fortunately there was another option available which avoided all the shortcomings mentioned above. This alternative was the use of the "Treasury Constant Maturity Series" as a benchmark. This series is compiled in the following manner.

At the close of each trading day, five leading U.S. Government securities dealers supply the Treasury with closing market-bid yields on all actively traded Treasury securities. The Treasury averages the five bid yields, unless one appears distinctly out of line, in which case it is discarded. These market yields are used to construct a daily yield curve from which the constant maturity yield values are read. This process permits, for example, the estimation of the yield on a ten-year security, even if no outstanding security actually has exactly ten years remaining to maturity.

Constant maturity values have been available throughout the 1980s on the three, six and twelve-month Treasury bills as well as on the two, three, five, seven, ten and thirty-year securities. No information is reported on the four-year constant maturity.

Using the change in the five-year and thirty-year constant maturity yields as the dependent variable resolves the problems mentioned earlier. The data displayed in Table 11 relate specifically to five-year constant maturity yields and Table 12 displays the comparable information on thirty-year constant maturity yields. In both tables, Column (1) shows the date of the auction under study and is labeled accordingly. This is followed by consecutively numbered columns showing the closing constant maturity yield the day before the auction (Day -1),the day of the auction (Day 0), the day following the auction (Day +1), three days following the auction (Day +3) and five days following the auction (Day +5). In all cases, the number of days refers to business days (excluding holidays).

TABLE 11

	CLOSING YIELDS					Col (3)-Col (2) BP Chg	Col (4)-Col (2) BP Chg	Col (5)-Col (2) BP Chg	Col (6)-Col (2) BP Chg
CONSTANT MATURITY YIELDS - FIVE YEAR									
AUCTION DATE (1)	DAY -1 (2)	DAY 0 (3)	DAY +1 (4)	DAY +3 (5)	DAY +5 (6)	(7)	(8)	(9)	(10)
						**	**	**	**
22680	13.70	14.12	14.08	13.48	13.61	0.42	0.38	-0.22	-0.09
60380	9.97	9.66	9.55	9.25	9.27	-0.31	-0.42	-0.72	-0.70
82780	11.55	11.76	11.92	11.45	11.15	0.21	0.37	-0.10	-0.40
120380	13.37	13.42	13.43	13.51	13.63	0.05	0.06	0.14	0.26
22681	13.61	13.80	13.76	13.78	13.78	0.19	0.15	0.17	0.17
502881	14.24	13.99	13.99	14.07	14.10	-0.25	-0.25	-0.17	-0.14
82781	15.99	16.15	16.01	16.09	16.17	0.16	0.02	0.10	0.18
112481	13.31	12.75	12.61	12.79	13.25	-0.56	-0.70	-0.52	-0.06
22482	14.03	13.98	14.01	13.97	13.77	-0.05	-0.02	-0.06	-0.26
52582	13.68	13.73	13.74	13.76	13.96	0.05	0.06	0.08	0.28
83182	12.71	12.65	12.58	12.26	12.40	-0.06	-0.13	-0.45	-0.31
112382	10.25	10.19	10.20	10.39	10.34	-0.06	-0.05	0.14	0.09
22383	10.01	10.00	9.96	9.83	9.76	-0.01	-0.05	-0.18	-0.25
60183	10.55	10.48	10.46	10.54	10.64	-0.07	-0.09	-0.01	0.09
83183	11.67	11.79	11.76	11.63	11.57	0.12	0.09	-0.04	-0.10
112983	11.41	11.31	11.36	11.47	11.46	-0.10	-0.05	0.06	0.05
22884	11.77	11.80	11.74	11.68	11.77	0.03	-0.03	-0.09	0.00
53184	13.84	13.76	13.46	13.24	13.43	-0.08	-0.38	-0.60	-0.41
82984	12.82	12.78	12.79	12.92	12.75	-0.04	-0.03	0.10	-0.07
112884	11.05	11.03	11.07	11.23	11.14	-0.02	0.02	0.18	0.09
22685	11.40	11.35	11.51	11.52	11.49	-0.05	0.11	0.12	0.09
52985	9.95	9.90	9.84	9.50	9.26	-0.05	-0.11	-0.45	-0.69
82885	9.65	9.63	9.58	9.71	9.71	-0.02	-0.07	0.06	0.06
112785	9.24	9.12	9.07	9.15	9.10	-0.12	-0.17	-0.09	-0.14
22686	8.21	8.07	7.91	7.76	7.76	-0.14	-0.30	-0.45	-0.45
52886	7.65	7.55	7.78	8.05	8.17	-0.10	0.13	0.40	0.52
82786	6.63	6.53	6.52	6.45	6.63	-0.10	-0.11	-0.18	0.00
112586	6.69	6.66	6.65	6.69	6.58	-0.03	-0.04	0.00	-0.11
22587	6.75	6.72	6.74	6.69	6.66	-0.03	-0.01	-0.06	-0.09
52787	8.23	8.28	8.25	8.08	8.25	0.05	0.02	-0.15	0.02
82887	8.48	8.54	8.52	8.77	8.82	0.06	0.04	0.29	0.34
112487	8.34	8.35	8.41	8.43	8.43	0.01	0.07	0.09	0.09
22588	7.69	7.68	7.67	7.61	7.59	-0.01	-0.02	-0.08	-0.10
52688	8.73	8.72	8.75	8.57	8.52	-0.01	0.02	-0.16	-0.21
82488	9.04	9.02	9.08	9.00	8.95	-0.02	0.04	-0.04	-0.09
112388	8.99	8.97	9.07	9.02	8.88	-0.02	0.08	0.03	-0.11
22389	9.43	9.47	9.49	9.42	9.38	0.04	0.06	-0.01	-0.05
52589	8.74	8.75	8.72	8.65	8.42	0.01	-0.02	-0.09	-0.32
82389	8.35	8.23	8.23	8.29	8.28	-0.12	-0.12	-0.06	-0.07
112989	7.81	7.78	7.74	7.70	7.76	-0.03	-0.07	-0.11	-0.05

** Indicates calculated field

Source: Federal Reserve Board, 1980-89, Various G.13 Releases.

TABLE 12

CONSTANT MATURITY YIELDS - THIRTY YEAR									
AUCTION DATE	CLOSING YIELDS					Col (3)-Col (2) BP Chg	Col (4)-Col (2) BP Chg	Col (5)-Col (2) BP Chg	Col (6)-Col (2) BP Chg
(1)	DAY -1 (2)	DAY 0 (3)	DAY +1 (4)	DAY +3 (5)	DAY +5 (6)	(7)	(8)	(9)	(10)
						**	**	**	**
20780	11.78	11.70	11.72	11.82	12.11	-0.08	-0.06	0.04	0.33
50880	10.19	10.34	10.41	10.29	10.46	0.15	0.22	0.10	0.27
80780	10.73	10.68	10.90	11.01	10.90	-0.05	0.17	0.28	0.17
110780	12.59	12.59	12.71	12.23	12.60	0.00	0.12	-0.36	0.01
20581	12.49	12.70	12.73	12.92	13.20	0.21	0.24	0.43	0.71
50781	13.97	13.84	13.76	13.95	13.66	-0.13	-0.21	-0.02	-0.31
80681	14.15	14.04	14.07	13.63	13.88	-0.11	-0.08	-0.52	-0.27
110581	13.96	14.06	13.85	13.55	13.26	0.10	-0.11	-0.41	-0.70
20482	14.41	14.54	14.43	14.80	14.54	0.13	0.02	0.39	0.13
110982	10.61	10.44	10.37	10.52	10.54	-0.17	-0.24	-0.09	-0.07
20383	10.94	11.06	11.12	11.12	10.96	0.12	0.18	0.18	0.02
50583	10.27	10.30	10.28	10.30	10.40	0.03	0.01	0.03	0.13
80483	11.87	12.12	12.07	12.09	12.00	0.25	0.20	0.22	0.13
111083	11.87	11.74	11.73	11.76	11.79	-0.13	-0.14	-0.11	-0.08
20984	11.83	11.84	11.92	11.92	12.02	0.01	0.09	0.09	0.19
51084	13.26	13.30	13.51	13.50	13.57	0.04	0.25	0.24	0.31
80984	12.62	12.47	12.47	12.48	12.51	-0.15	-0.15	-0.14	-0.11
110884	11.63	11.78	11.66	11.78	11.67	0.15	0.03	0.15	0.04
20785	11.37	11.29	11.27	11.31	11.37	-0.08	-0.10	-0.06	0.00
50985	11.39	11.34	11.20	11.07	11.02	-0.05	-0.19	-0.32	-0.37
80885	10.71	10.63	10.61	10.71	10.64	-0.08	-0.10	0.00	-0.07
112285	9.93	9.95	9.98	9.91	9.94	0.02	0.05	-0.02	0.01
20686	9.28	9.25	9.32	9.16	9.08	-0.03	0.04	-0.12	-0.20
50886	7.53	7.36	7.37	7.42	7.50	-0.17	-0.16	-0.11	-0.03
80786	7.57	7.56	7.41	7.34	7.29	-0.01	-0.16	-0.23	-0.28
110686	7.58	7.55	7.63	7.59	7.53	-0.03	0.05	0.01	-0.05
20587	7.51	7.47	7.47	7.61	7.59	-0.04	-0.04	0.10	0.08
50787	8.75	8.63	8.61	8.72	8.73	-0.12	-0.14	-0.03	-0.02
81387	8.95	8.85	8.77	8.95	8.94	-0.10	-0.18	0.00	-0.01
110587	8.92	8.80	8.85	8.88	8.93	-0.12	-0.07	-0.04	0.01
20488	8.39	8.46	8.36	8.40	8.40	0.07	-0.03	0.01	0.01
51288	9.22	9.17	9.11	9.22	9.30	-0.05	-0.11	0.00	0.08
111788	9.10	9.14	9.12	9.12	9.18	0.04	0.02	0.02	0.08
20989	8.82	8.99	9.05	9.10	9.06	0.17	0.23	0.28	0.24
51189	9.12	9.07	8.84	8.84	8.78	-0.05	-0.28	-0.28	-0.34
81089	8.12	8.08	8.13	8.19	8.16	-0.04	0.01	0.07	0.04
111489	7.89	7.90	7.87	7.94	7.91	0.01	-0.02	0.05	0.02

** Indicates calculated field

Source: Federal Reserve Board, 1980-89, Various G.13 Releases.

Columns (7)-(10) contain the key dependent variables used in this study. Column (7) is a calculated field which identifies the *basis point change* from the close of business the day before the auction (Day -1) compared to the close the day of the auction (Day 0). Due to the inverse relationship between bond yields and prices, a negative number implies rising prices. Column (8) displays the basis point change between the close of business the day following the auction (Day +1) with the day before the auction (Day -1). Column (9) displays the comparable change between (Day +3) and (Day -1) and Column (10) displays the change from (Day +5) compared to (Day - 1).

Data Collection Methods

The integrity of the data in a study such as this is of paramount importance. For that reason, the information displayed in Tables 9 and 10 was drawn directly from microfilm copies of the Department of Treasury news releases which occur late on the day of each auction. These microfilm copies were used to develop the information displayed in Tables 9 and 10.

The information displayed in Tables 11 and 12 on constant maturity yields have been available throughout the 1980s. The information used in the construction of Tables 11 and 12 was taken from microfilm copies of the monthly Federal Reserve G.13 Reports which display the constant maturity yields on a daily basis for three, six and twelve-month Treasury bills as well as two, three, five, seven, ten and thirty-year securities.

After assembling the data in Tables 9-12, the author undertook a thorough proofreading of all information. In addition, another independent reader also proofread all of the data displayed in those tables, thus assuring accuracy.

Identification and Interpretation: Key Variables

All columns of data reported on the independent variables identified in Tables 9 and 10 are of importance in this study; however, the previous research of Cammack and Wachtel identified the coverage ratio, tail and non-competitive percentage variables as most likely to show a relationship with the dependent variables identified in Tables 11 and 12.

In addition, the testing of the two New York District Federal Reserve data items also displayed in Tables 9 and 10 may be of assistance in answering the question posed herein. As far as this author could determine, this data had *not* been explored previously. These five independent variables identified in Tables 9 and 10 will be referred to as the "key" independent variables and therefore deserve further elaboration.

The "Coverage Ratio" is calculated by dividing Column (3) by Column (4). The markets have opposing interpretations of this ratio. One interpretation contends that strong demand leads to high coverage ratios and lower yields as the unsatisfied demand spills over into the secondary markets and pushes yields lower. Cammack's work in the Treasury Bill arena confirmed this effect as she found a tendency for secondary market prices to increase when the number of auction bidders was larger than expected (Cammack, 1987, 54).

The other interpretation contends that a large coverage ratio is symptomatic of investor uncertainty. Therefore, when the outcome of an auction is highly uncertain, sophisticated investors step up their use of "scale out" bids at progressively lower prices to gamble on purchasing the security at higher yields. This finding is confirmed by the work of Boatler (1985, 38) and Scott (1979, 280) who both found that primary dealers use "strip" bids in their bidding procedures for Treasury Bills. Their findings indicate that dealers, in particular, bid higher prices for securities which they genuinely desire to purchase and then scale their bids back so that additional securities are purchased only if "bargain" prices become available. This practice artificially inflates the number of tenders and thus boosts the coverage ratio. Wachtel also found evidence of this effect in his 1990 research on the impact of Treasury auction results on interest rates and refers to this as the "demand uncertainty" effect (Wachtel, 1990, 65).

The "Tail" of the issue is calculated by subtracting Column (7) from Column (6). Cammack (1987, 54) discovered with respect to Treasury Bill auctions that the tail seemed to indicate the degree of dispersion of opinion by investors as to the value of the security. Furthermore, she discovered that when the degree of dispersion is larger than expected there is a tendency for secondary market prices to drop. Wachtel's study also confirmed that large tails are typically associated with "sloppy" auctions where there is weak demand and wide dispersion of opinion about the value of the security. His work also confirmed Cammack's thesis that tails of this type are usually associated with higher yields in the secondary market (Wachtel, 1990, 69).

The percentage sold non-competitively is calculated by dividing Column (10) by Column (4). Wachtel discovered that a high percentage of purchase by small retail investors implied low demand by sophisticated institutional investors and dealers. Usually this event was associated with higher yields in the secondary market (Wachtel, 1990, 68).

New York District accepted bids as a percentage of the total issue sold are identified in Column (13). Two interpretations for these figures are possible. First, they serve as a proxy for primary dealer demand with large percentage purchases by New York dealers indicating a strong demand for the security by dealers and lower secondary market yields. Or, as previously mentioned, it may show a great deal of uncertainty regarding the market with dealers placing a large number of "scale out" bids gambling on "cheap" prices. Under this condition the market would likely gravitate to higher yields.

Column (15) displays the New York District accepted bids as a percentage of the New York District tenders. This figure provides a truer indication of how effectively demand by the dealer community has been satisfied in the auction. When dealers do not obtain the necessary securities desired in the auction (as indicated by a low percentage), they are forced to carry those unsatisfied demands into the secondary market, thus pressuring prices higher and yields lower.

The dependent variables for this study are identified in Tables 11 and 12. Although all of the data are important, the most critical information relates to the basis point change columns which are Columns (7)-(10). These columns indicate the change which occurred in the market throughout each auction period. These variables, identified in Columns (7)-(10), shall be referred to as "key" dependent variables.

Research Design and Statistical Approach

The design of this study involved calculating descriptive statistics using the "key" independent variables identified in Tables 9 and 10 and the "key" dependent variables identified in Tables 11 and 12. These statistics consisting of mean, median, maximum, minimum, standard deviation, range, coefficient of skewness and variation values were then used in determining outliers and data normality.

For this study an outlier was defined as a data point lying more than three standard deviations from the respective mean. In determining the normality of the data, the Pearson skewness coefficient was employed. The skewness coefficient has a range of +3 to -3, and research indicates that when the skewness coefficient is between +1 and -1, an approximation to normality of the data can be assumed (Brykit, 1979, 45). The issue of normality was important in determining the analytical technique most suitable for answering the research question.

According to Mulligan, in determining which analytical technique to use in testing such a hypothesis, the following factors need to be considered:

1) the time into the future that must be forecast,
2) the degree of accuracy required,
3) the lead time needed before making the decision,
4) the quality of the data available,
5) the benefits expected from a successful forecast and
6) the costs associated with using a particular technique
(Mulligan 1989, 478).

The research approach which met the above criteria was a correlational design using linear regression.

Linear regression is a technique used to determine whether and by how much a change in one independent variable will result in a change in a dependent variable (Valentine, 1971, 77). Using this technique, the key independent variables identified in Columns (5), (9), (11), (13) and (15) of Tables 9 and 10 were regressed against the key dependent variables displayed in Columns (7)-(10) of Tables 11 and 12. Primary emphasis was placed on Column (7) in testing the hypothesis. When statistical significance was in evidence, follow up testing using Columns (8)-(10) was undertaken. By this means, auction results as predictors of near-term interest rate movements was tested.

The size and sign of the calculated coefficients of each regression equation were studied to determine their importance in answering the research question. Once each regression was completed, the statistical "t" test was used to test for the significance of the coefficient. Attention was also directed to (R^2), the coefficient of determination, which measures the proportion of total variation in the dependent variable "Y" that is explained by the independent variable "X" (Mason, 1990, 571). In general, an R^2 of .50 is considered moderate correlation, with values approaching 1.0 indicative of strong correlation.

Using this research design and statistical approach, the feasibility of using some or all of the information contained in Treasury auction releases to predict near-term interest rate movements was determined.

Given the sample size and volatile time frame used in the study, it was determined that the results of this study could be applied to the entire spectrum of Treasury note and bonds. Wachtel's 1990 work mentioned earlier in this study supports this position as he found very little disparity in the results of a six-year study between the various auctions which were incorporated therein (Wachtel 1990, 69).

FINDINGS

Descriptive Statistics - Independent Variables

The descriptive statistics applied to the independent variables used in this study are displayed on the following pages in tabular form. These data represent preliminary observations undertaken *prior to regressing*. This is important since normality of the data is a prerequisite to the use of regression analysis.

Table 13 shows the key independent variable data which corresponds to the five-year auction results originally displayed in Table 9. After compiling this data, one outlying data point was identified and the descriptive statistics were recomputed and displayed in Table 14. In this case, the outlier was an 11 basis point tail occurring on February 26, 1980.

The comparable descriptive data on the thirty-year auction results originally shown in Table 10 are displayed in Table 15. After compiling this data, two outlying data points were identified thus generating the information in Table 16. The two outliers were a 14 basis point tail which occurred on November 5, 1981 and a 4.19 coverage ratio which occurred on November 5, 1987.

An analysis of the information in Tables 13 and 14 reveals several important points. First, the skewness coefficients computed in Table 13 clearly conform to the normal approximation. Exclusion of the one outlying data point does not substantially improve the normality of the data. Therefore, *all* data were included and normality of the data was assumed.

A similar result is clear when comparing Table 15 and Table 16. Excluding the two outliers does not improve the normality of the results, therefore once again *all* data were included. One of the five variables had a skewness coefficient of -1.21, but since the deviation was not significantly larger than -1.00, the data was again assumed to be normal.

TABLE 13

FIVE YEAR AUCTION RESULTS

DESCRIPTIVE STATISTICS
KEY INDEPENDENT VARIABLES - ALL DATA

	COVERAGE RATIO (5)	TAIL BPs (9)	NCOMPS as % TOTAL (11)	NYFDACC as % TOTSLD (13)	NYFDACC as %APPL (15)
	(40 observations)			(37 observations)	
MEAN	2.58	1.70	10.3	88.1	39.9
MEDIAN	2.56	1.00	8.8	89.0	39.6
MAXIMUM	3.50	11.00	22.7	96.0	56.0
MINIMUM	1.67	0.00	3.1	71.8	27.1
STD DEVIATION	0.45	2.12	5.6	5.7	6.8
RANGE	1.83	11.00	19.6	24.2	28.9
COEFFICIENT OF:					
SKEWNESS	+.13	+.99	+.80	-.47	+.13
VARIATION	0.17	1.25	0.54	0.06	0.17

Source: Table 9; all calculated fields
( ) denotes specific column location in Table 9.

TABLE 14

FIVE YEAR AUCTION RESULTS

DESCRIPTIVE STATISTICS
KEY INDEPENDENT VARIABLES - EXCLUDING OUTLIER

	COVERAGE RATIO (5)	TAIL BPs (9)	NCOMPS as % TOTAL (11)	NYFDACC as % TOTSLD (13)	NYFDACC as%APPL (15)
	(39 observations)			(37 observations)	
MEAN	2.60	1.46	10.3	88.1	39.9
MEDIAN	2.56	1.00	8.7	89.0	39.6
MAXIMUM	3.50	7.00	22.7	96.0	56.0
MINIMUM	1.67	0.00	3.1	71.8	27.1
STD DEVIATION	0.44	1.53	5.6	5.7	6.8
RANGE	1.83	7.00	19.6	24.2	28.9
COEFFICIENT OF:					
SKEWNESS	+.27	+.90	+.86	-.47	+.13
VARIATION	0.17	1.05	0.55	0.06	0.17

Source: Table 9; all calculated fields

( ) denotes specific column location in Table 9.

TABLE 15

THIRTY YEAR AUCTION RESULTS

DESCRIPTIVE STATISTICS
KEY INDEPENDENT VARIABLES - ALL DATA

	COVERAGE RATIO (5)	TAIL BPs (9)	NCOMPS as % TOTAL (11)	NYFDACC as % TOTSLD (13)	NYFDACC as%APPL (15)
	(37 observations)			(34 observations)	
MEAN	2.29	2.62	8.7	91.7	46.3
MEDIAN	2.20	2.00	7.1	93.4	47.7
MAXIMUM	4.19	14.00	24.6	96.0	66.3
MINIMUM	1.54	0.00	2.2	79.5	24.7
STD DEVIATION	0.51	2.68	6.3	4.2	8.5
RANGE	2.65	14.00	22.4	16.5	41.6
COEFFICIENT OF:					
SKEWNESS	+.53	+.69	+.76	-1.21	-.49
VARIATION	0.22	1.02	0.72	0.05	0.18

Source: Table 10; all calculated fields

( ) denotes specific column location in Table 10.

TABLE 16

THIRTY YEAR AUCTION RESULTS

DESCRIPTIVE STATISTICS
KEY INDEPENDENT VARIABLES - EXCLUDING OUTLIERS

	COVERAGE RATIO (5)	TAIL BPs (9)	NCOMPS % TOTAL (11)	NYFDACC as % TOTSLD (13)	NYFDACC as%APPL (15)
	(35 observations)			(32 observations)	
MEAN	2.26	2.37	8.8	91.8	46.4
MEDIAN	2.18	2.00	6.5	93.8	47.8
MAXIMUM	3.47	9.00	24.6	96.0	59.2
MINIMUM	1.66	0.00	2.2	79.5	30.3
STD DEVIATION	0.39	1.91	6.4	4.0	7.1
RANGE	1.80	9.00	22.4	16.5	28.9
COEFFICIENT OF:					
SKEWNESS	+.62	+.58	+1.08	-1.50	-.59
VARIATION	0.17	0.81	0.73	0.04	0.15

Source: Table 10; all calculated fields

( ) denotes specific column location in Table 10.

Several other interesting points were observed about the information in Tables 13 and 15. First, the coverage ratios between the two sets of auction data are not substantially different.

However the tail of the issues diverges compared with the other independent variables. First, the coefficient of variation on both five-year and thirty-year results shows substantially more variation in this independent variable than any others identified. Also, the thirty-year tail mean is nearly a full basis point larger than the five-year tail mean.

As previously noted, the tail is a proxy for the degree of dispersion of opinion by investors as to the value of the security. The results would indicate that overall, thirty-year auction bids contain more divergence of opinion than five-year auction bids.

The non-competitive percentage indicates that individuals participate more actively in five-year note sales than thirty-year bond sales. Conversely, primary dealers purchase more of the thirty-year security than of the five-year security. Finally, dealers are able to satisfy more of their demand for securities in the thirty-year auction than in the five-year auction. This is apparent when examining Column (15) in Tables 13 and 15.

Descriptive Statistics - Dependent Variables

The descriptive statistics on the dependent variables used in this study are displayed on the following pages in tabular form. These data represent preliminary observations undertaken *prior to regressing*. This is important information since normality of the data is a prerequisite to the use of regression analysis.

Table 17 describes all five-year data related to the key dependent variables identified earlier in Table 11. After compiling these data, one outlying data point was identified. The descriptive statistics were recomputed and displayed in Table 18. In this case, the outlying data point was identified as a 56 basis point decline in yield between Day -1 and Day 0 on November 24, 1981.

The comparable descriptive data on the thirty-year auction results originally displayed in Table 12 are displayed in Tables 19 and 20. In this case, no outliers were identified; therefore, the information in Tables 19 and 20 is identical.

TABLE 17

FIVE YEAR AUCTION RESULTS

DESCRIPTIVE STATISTICS
KEY DEPENDENT VARIABLES - ALL DATA

(40 observations)

	DAY 0 vs DAY -1 BPs (7)	DAY +1 vs DAY -1 BPs (8)	DAY +3 vs DAY -1 BPs (9)	DAY +5 vs DAY -1 BPs (10)
MEAN	-2.65	-3.80	-7.82	-7.35
MEDIAN	-2.00	-2.00	-6.00	-7.00
MAXIMUM	42.00	38.00	40.00	52.00
MINIMUM	-56.00	-70.00	-72.00	-70.00
STD DEVIATION	14.70	18.62	23.29	24.59
RANGE	98.00	108.00	112.00	112.00
COEFFICIENT OF:				
SKEWNESS	-.13	-.29	-.23	-.04
VARIATION	5.55	4.90	2.98	3.35

Source: Table 11; all calculated fields

( ) denotes specific column location in Table 11.

TABLE 18

FIVE YEAR AUCTION RESULTS

DESCRIPTIVE STATISTICS
KEY DEPENDENT VARIABLES - EXCLUDING OUTLIER

(39 observations)

	DAY 0 vs DAY -1 BPs (7)	DAY +1 vs DAY -1 BPs (8)	DAY +3 vs DAY -1 BPs (9)	DAY +5 vs DAY -1 BPs (10)
MEAN	-1.28	-2.10	-7.82	-7.35
MEDIAN	-2.00	-2.00	-6.00	-7.00
MAXIMUM	42.00	38.00	40.00	52.00
MINIMUM	-31.00	-42.00	-72.00	-70.00
STD DEVIATION	12.12	15.51	23.29	24.59
RANGE	73.00	80.00	112.00	112.00
COEFFICIENT OF:				
SKEWNESS	+.18	-.02	-.23	-.04
VARIATION	9.47	7.39	2.98	3.35

Source: Table 11; all calculated fields

( ) denotes specific column location in Table 11.

TABLE 19

THIRTY YEAR AUCTION RESULTS

DESCRIPTIVE STATISTICS
KEY DEPENDENT VARIABLES - ALL DATA

(37 Observations)

	DAY 0 vs DAY -1 BPs (7)	DAY +1 vs DAY -1 BPs (8)	DAY +3 vs DAY -1 BPs (9)	DAY +5 vs DAY -1 BPs (10)
MEAN	-0.78	-1.73	-0.45	0.27
MEDIAN	-3.00	-3.00	0.00	1.00
MAXIMUM	25.00	25.00	43.00	71.00
MINIMUM	-17.00	-28.00	-52.00	-70.00
STD DEVIATION	10.76	14.38	20.58	23.48
RANGE	42.00	53.00	95.00	141.00
COEFFICIENT OF:				
SKEWNESS	+0.62	+0.26	-.07	-.09
VARIATION	13.79	8.31	45.73	86.96

Source: Table 12; all calculated fields

( ) denotes specific column location in Table 12.

TABLE 20

THIRTY YEAR AUCTION RESULTS

DESCRIPTIVE STATISTICS
KEY DEPENDENT VARIABLES - EXCLUDING OUTLIERS

(37 Observations)

	DAY 0 vs DAY -1 BPs (7)	DAY +1 vs DAY -1 BPs (8)	DAY +3 vs DAY -1 BPs (9)	DAY +5 vs DAY -1 BPs (10)
MEAN	-0.78	-1.73	-0.45	0.27
MEDIAN	-3.00	-3.00	0.00	1.00
MAXIMUM	25.00	25.00	43.00	71.00
MINIMUM	-17.00	-28.00	-52.00	-70.00
STD DEVIATION	10.76	14.38	20.58	23.48
RANGE	42.00	53.00	95.00	141.00
COEFFICIENT OF:				
SKEWNESS	+0.62	+0.26	-.07	-.09
VARIATION	13.79	8.31	45.73	86.96

Source: Table 12; all calculated fields

( ) denotes specific column location in Table 12.

An analysis of the information in Tables 17 and 18 reveals several important points. First, the skewness coefficients computed in Table 17 clearly conform to the normal approximation mentioned above. Exclusion of the one outlying data point does not substantially improve the normality of the data. Therefore, inclusion of *all* data was determined more appropriate than selective deletion of data.

Table 19 also indicates that normality of the data are approximated and since no outliers were identified, *all* of the data were used.

Since the distributions of both independent and dependent variables approximated normality, the linear regression results described below were considered *valid* for the purpose of this study.

Several other observations about the information in Tables 17-20 are worthy of note. First, the coefficient of variation noted with respect to the thirty-year auction results is substantially larger than for the five-year results. As noted earlier, this variation is linked to the dispersion of opinion as to the value of the security.

Second, although subject to great variability, the market *generally* rallies during and immediately following both five and thirty-year auctions. An examination of the mean and median basis point change in both Tables 17 and 19 highlights this fact. The negative numbers indicate lower yields and thus higher bond prices during the study period. The results shown in Table 17 indicate the five-year note in particular *gains* upward price momentum following the auction. On the other hand, the strength displayed during and after the thirty-year auctions dissipates much more quickly (See Table 19).

Regression Results - Five Year Auctions

The results of the regression tests are located in Appendix A, Tables A-1 through A-10. In cases where the independent variable was expressed as a percentage, the dependent variable was also converted to a percentage prior to regressing. These results have been summarized and displayed in Tables 21 and 22. Table 21 is drawn from Tables A-1 through A-5 and displays the regression results of the five key independent variables already identified. In this table, they are individually regressed against Column (7) of Table 11. This dependent variable is the market change from the closing levels the day before the auction compared to the close the day of the

TABLE 21

FIVE YEAR AUCTION RESULTS - ALL DATA

REGRESSION SUMMARY TABLE
Dependent Variable (Y): Table 11; Column (7)

Key Independent Variables (Xs)	Calculated Coefficents	R sqd	Computed "t"	Significant
Coverage Ratio	-0.02078	0.004	0.3929	No
Tail	0.0198	0.08	1.8394	Yes @ 10%
Non Comp %	0.007902	0.001	0.2234	No
NY Acc % Ttl	-0.00625	0.001	0.216	No
NY Acc % Appl	0.003603	0.0006	0.1481	No

Source: Tables A1 - A5.

TABLE 22

FIVE YEAR AUCTION RESULTS - ALL DATA

REGRESSION SUMMARY TABLE
Dependent Variable (Y): Table 11; Column (8)

Key Independent Variables (Xs)	Calculated Coefficents	R sqd	Computed "t"	Significant
Coverage Ratio	0.0201	0.002	0.3006	No
Tail	0.0114	0.017	0.811	No
Non Comp %	-0.0203	0.005	0.4341	No
NY Acc % Ttl	0.0212	0.008	0.5347	No
NY Acc % Appl	-0.0071	0.001	0.212	No

Source: Tables A6 - A10.

auction. The computed value of "t" was used to test for the significance of each coefficient and, as noted in the Table 21, only the tail coefficient displayed significance at the 10 percent level with an R^2 of 0.08. Since the sign of this coefficient was positive, it implies that large tails are associated with positive yield changes. Given bond market mathematics, this further implies falling secondary bond market prices. This finding parallels Cammack's 1987 work in the Treasury bill market and Wachtel's 1990 findings in the broader note and bond markets.

A further test was conducted to determine if the significance noted in Table 21 carried through to the next trading day. The same independent variables were regressed against Column (8) of Table 11, comparing the change from the close the day prior to the auction (Day -1) with the close the day *after* the auction (Day +1). These results are shown in Tables A-6 through A-10 and are summarized in Table 22. They indicate that with the passage of one trading day the significance of the tail coefficient is lost. This result is not particularly startling since the markets are constantly bombarded with new information. Any unexpected piece of news during that twenty-four hour period could cause the significance of the coefficient to be lost.

Regression Results - Thirty Year Auctions

The results of the regression tests on the thirty-year bond are located in Appendix B, Tables B-1 through B-12. When the independent variable was expressed as a percentage, the dependent variable was converted to a percentage prior to regressing. These results are summarized and displayed as Tables 23-25.

Table 23 is drawn from Tables B-1 through B-5 and displays the regression results of the five key independent variables already identified. In this table, they are individually regressed against Column (7) of Table 12. This dependent variable is the market change from the closing levels the day before the auction (Day -1) compared to the close the day of the auction (Day 0). The computed value of "t" was used to test for the significance of each coefficient. Significance was again discovered with respect to the tail, as noted in the five-year results. Stronger significance was discovered with respect to the coverage ratio coefficient. Very strong significance, as well as

TABLE 23

THIRTY YEAR AUCTION RESULTS - ALL DATA

REGRESSION SUMMARY TABLE
Dependent Variable (Y): Table 12; Column (7)

Key Independent Variables (Xs)	Calculated Coefficents	R sqd	Computed "t"	Significant
Coverage Ratio	-0.10258	0.23318	3.26242	Yes @ 1%
Tail	0.013349	0.110933	2.1111	Yes @ 5%
Non Comp %	0.02492	0.023648	0.920728	No
NY Acc % Ttl	-0.03741	0.023526	0.87806	No
NY Acc % Appl	0.065787	0.30419	3.740265	Yes @ .1%

Source: Tables B1 - B5.

TABLE 24

THIRTY YEAR AUCTION RESULTS - ALL DATA

REGRESSION SUMMARY TABLE
Dependent Variable (Y): Table 12; Column (8)

Key Independent Variables (Xs)	Calculated Coefficents	R sqd	Computed "t"	Significant
Coverage Ratio	-0.10072	0.12573	2.24352	Yes @ 5%
Tail	0.013153	0.060221	1.4976	No
Non Comp %	0.024143	0.0118878	0.648907	No
NY Acc % Ttl	-0.00831	0.00066	0.14548	No
NY Acc % Appl	0.052407	0.10984	1.98711	Yes @ 10%

Source: Tables B6 - B10.

TABLE 25

THIRTY YEAR AUCTION RESULTS - ALL DATA

REGRESSION SUMMARY TABLE
Dependent Variable (Y): Table 12; Column (9)

Key Independent Variables (Xs)	Calculated Coefficents	R sqd	Computed "t"	Significant
Coverage Ratio	-0.04773	0.0136	0.69984	No
NY Acc % Appl	0.0168494	0.006515	0.458106	No

Source: Tables B11 - B12.

a relatively high R^2, was discovered with respect to the New York District acceptance/application ratio.

The tail coefficient sign was positive. As mentioned in relation to the five-year results, a large tail is associated with a positive yield shift and lower secondary market prices. This reconfirms the work of both Cammack and Wachtel.

The coverage ratio's coefficient was negative indicating that large coverage ratios are associated with small or negative yield changes and higher secondary bond market prices. This confirms Cammack's finding relative to Treasury bill auctions.

The New York District acceptance/application ratio generated a positive coefficient. This suggests that when dealers purchase a large portion of the securities *for which they bid*, their demands are satisfied; therefore, the lack of secondary market dealer buying allows prices to erode and yields drift higher.

A further test was conducted to determine if the significance noted in Table 23 carried through to the next trading day. The same independent variables were regressed against Column (8) of Table 12 thus comparing the close the day prior to the auction (Day -1) with the close the day after the auction (Day +1). These results are shown in Tables B-6 through B-10 and are summarized in Table 24. These results indicate that the significance of the tail coefficient is lost. However, the other two coefficients remain significant and their respective signs remain unchanged.

Given the results noted in Table 24, the two remaining independent variables were tested for significance relative to Column (9) of Table 12 and displayed in Table 25. The significance of these final two coefficients is lost when (Day +3) data are compared with (Day -1) data. This again is not particularly startling given the wide range of information which constantly bombards the securities markets on a daily basis.

Regression Results - Extreme Observations

The 1990 work of Wachtel contained an interesting and instructive approach to answering a research question similar to the one posed here. Wachtel addressed the issue of extreme observations or "surprises," as he referred to them. He hypothesized that market participants deal constantly with uncertainty; therefore, they would only react to abnormal events that he categorized as surprises.

Using his hypothesis, a correlation between the independent and dependent variables in this study would more likely occur when the independent variables were considered to be surprises by the market.

In order to test Wachtel's thesis using data from this study, the key concern was the definition of a surprise. Wachtel defined surprises as the data points which were outside one standard deviation from the mean. Using this definition, an excessive number of data points were excluded from this study. Therefore, a modified definition was employed, and surprises were defined as data points falling outside *one-half standard deviation* from the mean.

Using this approach, additional regressions were undertaken, the results of which appear in Tables 26-30. Tables 26 and 27 are drawn from the results shown in Appendix C and display the five-year data. Tables 28-30 are drawn from the results shown in Appendix D and display the thirty-year data.

In examining Tables 26 and 27, the five-year regression results obtained using this revised methodology were largely the same as those noted in Tables 21 and 22. In short, the tail again showed significance at the 10 percent level when (Day -1) was compared to (Day 0). The significance was lost however when (Day -1) was compared to (Day +1). More importantly, the R^2 relative to the tail coefficient doubled from .08 to .171. This indicates that the modified methodology has much better explanatory power than detected in the previous regressions, although still quite low in absolute terms. It also tends to confirm Wachtel's surprise hypothesis.

An examination of Tables 28-30 also reveals some interesting facts. In these tables, the results of the comparable thirty-year regressions are shown. Some results were similar to those shown earlier in Tables 23-25. For example, significance was found with the coverage ratio, the tail and the New York District acceptance/application ratio when (Day -1) was compared to (Day 0). Significance weakened substantially when (Day -1) was compared to (Day +1). Significance virtually disappeared earlier when (Day -1) was compared to (Day +3). These findings correlate strongly with the results noted earlier in Tables 23-25.

TABLE 26

FIVE YEAR AUCTION RESULTS

REGRESSION SUMMARY TABLE

Dependent Variable (Y): Table 11; Column (7)
Data Points -.5 SD < & > +.5 SD from Mean

Key Independent Variables (Xs)	Calculated Coefficents	R sqd	Computed "t"	Significant
Coverage Ratio	-0.02	0.00724	0.4184	No
Tail	0.02076	0.1715	1.8759	Yes @ 10%
Non Comp %	0.0145	0.00667	0.40155	No
NY Acc % Ttl	-0.0036	0.00106	0.1496	No
NY Acc % Appl	0.00479	0.00358	0.00011	No

Source: Tables C1 - C5.

TABLE 27

FIVE YEAR AUCTION RESULTS

REGRESSION SUMMARY TABLE

Dependent Variable (Y): Table 11; Column (8)
Data Points -.5 SD < & > +.5 SD> from Mean

Key Independent Variable (X)	Calculated Coefficents	R sqd	Computed "t"	Significant
Tail	0.0113	0.0382	0.822	No

Source: Table C6.

TABLE 28

THIRTY YEAR AUCTION RESULTS

REGRESSION SUMMARY TABLE
Data points -.5 SD < and > +.5 SD from Mean
Dependent Variable (Y): Table 12; Column (7)

Key Independent Variables (Xs)	Calculated Coefficents	R sqd	Computed "t"	Significant
Coverage Ratio	-0.1054	0.5907	4.652	Yes @ .1%
Tail	0.01385	0.2509	2.588	Yes @ 2%
Non Comp %	0.02162	0.0258	0.7471	No
NY Acc % Ttl	-0.0343	0.0211	0.7361	No
NY Acc % Appl	0.07126	0.6919	6.179	Yes @ .1%

Source: Tables D1 - D5.

TABLE 29

THIRTY YEAR AUCTION RESULTS

REGRESSION SUMMARY TABLE
Data points -.5 SD < and > +.5 SD from Mean
Dependent Variable (Y): Table 12; Column (8)

Key Independent Variables (Xs)	Calculated Coefficents	R sqd	Computed "t"	Significant
Coverage Ratio	-0.10378	0.298	2.5234	Yes @ 5%
Tail	0.01368	0.1171	1.629	No
NY Acc % Appl	0.0593	0.2848	2.601	Yes @ 2%

Source: Tables D6 - D8.

TABLE 30

THIRTY YEAR AUCTION RESULTS

REGRESSION SUMMARY TABLE
Data points -.5 SD < and > +.5 SD from Mean
Dependent Variable (Y): Table 12; Column (9)

Key Independent Variables (Xs)	Calculated Coefficents	R sqd	Computed "t"	Significant
Coverage Ratio	-0.0448	0.021	0.568	No
NY Acc % Appl	0.016	0.0097	0.4096	No

Source: Tables D9 - D11.

However, interesting differences also surfaced, primarily with respect to the R^2 calculation. With the modified methodology displayed in Tables 28-30, the R^2s on all significant variables *increased dramatically*. For example, R^2 increased from .23 to .59 on the coverage ratio, from .11 to .25 on the tail and from .30 to .69 on the New York District acceptance/application ratio. This indicates a dramatic increase in the explanatory power of the variation in the dependent variable which is explained by the three independent variables. Clearly the New York District acceptance/application coefficient offers the most explanatory power of the variables studied. As noted with respect to the five-year results displayed in Tables 26 and 27, these results also strongly reinforce Wachtel's surprise hypothesis.

In summary, these results seem to corroborate the Wachtel hypothesis. Traders and portfolio managers continually operate in an environment of uncertainty and volatility. Given the demands of this type of environment, sophisticated investors often ignore Treasury auction information which is not dramatically different from "expectation." Information which differs substantially from the "norm" is much more useful in forecasting near-term interest rate movements.

IMPLICATIONS

The focus of this study was to determine if an analysis of U.S. Treasury auction results could be used to predict near-term interest rate movements. The previous four chapters have served to introduce the subject, examine and critique the relevant literature, explain the methodology which was used in the study and present the findings.

The final section of this document is devoted to answering the research question and addressing several peripheral yet important issues which have surfaced during the course of this research effort.

Implications for Fixed-Income Traders and Portfolio Managers

Given the results of this research, several recommendations can be made to fixed-income participants about using U.S. Treasury auction results as an aid in forecasting near-term interest rate movements.

First, of the five key independent auction variables identified in this study, two can be eliminated as completely insignificant for forecasting purposes. The non-competitive percentage and New York District acceptance/total sold ratio showed no correlation to the market change variables.

Second, the use of five-year auction data must be strictly confined to the use of the tail for forecasting future interest rates (See Table 21). As confirmed by both Wachtel (1990) and Cammack (1987), large tails are associated with a high degree of investor uncertainty and thus higher yields and lower bond prices typically follow. This finding is confirmed by the positive coefficient and significant "t" value found when (Day -1) is compared to (Day 0). Caution must be used when applying these data since the significance level was demonstrated at only 10 percent and the R^2 was calculated at only .08. Furthermore, even this weak significance disappears with the passage of one additional trading day. In short, correlation and significance do exist but they are weak and fleeting in nature.

Third, thirty-year auction results contain more useful information when forecasting interest rates (See Tables 23 and 24). The coverage ratio, tail and New York District acceptance/application ratio displayed significance at the 1 percent, 5 percent and .1 percent level respectively, when comparing the market change from the day before the auction to the day of the auction. The R^2s are all substantially higher than the comparable five-year coefficients of determination, although not particularly high in an absolute sense. More importantly, the significance of the coverage ratio and New York District acceptance/application ratio carry through to the following trading day, although weakened in strength.

The signs of the respective coefficients are also instructive. The negative sign of the coverage ratio indicates that large coverage ratios are associated with negative yield shifts and higher bond prices. This confirms the earlier work of Cammack (1987). The positive tail coefficient result indicates that large tails are associated with investor uncertainty and positive yield shifts (i.e. lower bond prices). This confirms the work of both Cammack (1987) and Wachtel (1990).

The previously unexplored New York District acceptance/application ratio generated a positive coefficient. This suggests that large purchases as a percentage of applications by primary dealers are associated with positive yield shifts and downward movements in bond prices. This effect apparently occurs because primary dealers have satisfied their demand for the security in the auction process, consequently there is a lack of follow-up buying, which allows prices to erode and yields to be pushed higher.

Finally, although the information contained in the thirty-year auction results is much more instructive than the comparable five-year data, the modest R^2s show that much of the variation in the dependent variable is unexplained by the independent variable. To further explore this relationship, Wachtel's surprise methodology was used as explained previously in detail. In short, using data points that are one-half standard deviation or more away from the mean nearly doubled the R^2 on the five-year results.

The change in the comparable thirty-year data was even more dramatic as noted earlier and displayed in Tables 28 and 29. The level of significance increased measurably, and the corresponding R^2s either doubled or tripled in magnitude, depending on the specific independent variable.

As Wachtel noted, this result has important implications for traders and portfolio managers. Since the markets are an uncertain operating environment, unless an auction result deviates somewhat from "normal" expectations, it will be ignored by the market. Therefore, market participants should pay particular attention to auction results which fall outside the "normal" range of expectation. Furthermore, given the moderately high R^2s displayed in Table 28, participants should focus their attention on the thirty-year coverage ratio and *particularly* on the New York District acceptance/application ratio when data extremes are evident. This is recommended since the latter variable has not been researched before.

Given the results in Tables 21-30, it is clear that beside the issues of significance and correlation strength, the question of time frame must also be addressed.

In examining the five-year results, it is clear that any significance which did exist on the day of the auction (Day 0) is gone by the close the day after the auction (Day +1). This suggests that to use the results profitably, market participants must react between the time the auction results are released late in the trading day and the close of trading. Depending upon the time of the press release this is often no more than a few minutes.

With the thirty-year results, since significance was still evident on Day +1, market participants have more reaction time. They have the "luxury" of pondering the results of the significant variables overnight and into the following trading day, acting at an opportune moment before the close.

In either case, aggressive short term traders, arbitragers, primary dealers and speculators are most likely to find this information valuable. Portfolio managers typically plan over a much longer time frame and will likely find this information too short term in nature to be helpful.

Efficient Market Implications

This study was not designed to assess the efficiency of the U.S. government securities market. However, during this research some interesting and unexpected findings resulted related to this topic.

By way of background, the "strong form" of the efficient market hypothesis states that current bond or stock market prices reflect all pertinent information, publicly or privately held. Proponents of the strong-form hypothesis believe that a simple "no change" market forecast is as likely to be accurate as a forecast produced by the "experts." In fact, the findings of Pesando (1981), Fraser (1977) and Prell (1973) all confirmed this strong-form thesis with respect to the government bond markets.

This study verifies that the five-year Treasury sector is highly efficient and conforms to the strong-form hypothesis. This is the case since the information contained in the five-year auction results is of limited usefulness. Possession of these auction results before their official release would still offer the investor very little profit opportunity. This finding is not particularly startling since the short-term Treasury markets have been characterized as "efficient" for some time.

More interesting are the efficiency implications of the thirty-year Treasury sector. Thirty-year auction results, particularly data extremes, *are* useful in forecasting near-term interest rate movements. Therefore, some market inefficiency is implied. Possession of data relating to thirty-year auction results would provide the trader with information which could be used in the production of reasonably accurate near-term interest rate forecasts (within the statistical limitations earlier discussed). Thus there appears to be a difference in efficiency characteristics between the intermediate and long term sector of the Treasury market. Market participants have suspected this for some time and these results tend to confirm that suspicion.

If the thirty-year Treasury sector is relatively inefficient, then profit opportunities exist for traders and investors who are aware of fundamental or technical indicators which can produce consistently high quality interest rate forecasts. This premise is true regardless of whether the trader is using auction results or other indicators not included in this research as the basis for the forecast. In short, profit

nally, the dramatic new results discovered relative to the New
strict acceptance/application ratio warrant additional work.
dy demonstrated the significance of this ratio with respect to
ty-year bond but not the five-year note. It would be an
ng exercise to determine the significance of this ratio with
to the rest of the Treasury yield curve.

ny of these recommendations for future research offer
. Hopefully, the new information discovered in this study will
useful to those who wish to move forward in a similar
n.

opportunities exist in the thirty-year market which are not available
in the short to intermediate sectors of that same market.

Primary Dealer Collusion

Although not specifically the focus of this research effort,
recent events related to collusion in the auction process merit
additional discussion. Since primary government dealers are heavily
involved in U.S. Treasury auctions (See Tables 13 and 15), the issue
of collusion between those dealers is of importance in confirming the
integrity of these findings.

A definition of collusion is in order as the term tends to be
used quite loosely. Collusion can be defined as a secret agreement
among sellers to fix prices, divide the market or in some other way
limit competition (Rohlf 1989, 196). As applied to the government
securities market, the term "seller" refers to a primary dealer. In this
scenario, collusion refers to an attempt by primary dealers to "fix" the
price of the security being bought from the U.S. Treasury and profit
from it's resale to the retail or institutional market.

As mentioned earlier, the evidence on collusion between
primary dealers before 1990 is quite mixed. Boatler (1985) found
evidence of collusion in his Treasury bill study covering 1952-59.
However, in a similar study Michael Reiber (1965) found collusion to
be "highly unlikely." Finally, Milton Freidman's 1963 research found
an incentive to collude but *no evidence of actual collusion*.

Recent Wall Street Journal articles have contended that
collusion has long been practiced by primary dealers (Siconolfi
August 19, 1991, p.A1). However, in these articles the authors
typically define collusion as the discussion of *possible* bidding
strategies before the actual auction. This is indeed done by primary
dealers and institutional investors alike but this action is *not*
necessarily illegal, according to some securities lawyers (Cohen
September 16, 1991, p.C1). With the electronic technology of today
and when-issued trading, the market value of the soon-to-be-
auctioned security is plainly visible to all primary dealers as well as
thousands of institutional investors. According to John Coffee Jr.,
professor of securities law at Columbia University, to actually prove
collusion the government must show that firms have conspired with

each other to restrain trade or manipulate the market (Cohen October 7, 1991, p.A10). This distinction is critical and yet is misunderstood. This misunderstanding has led to the current misconceptions regarding collusion.

The following facts support this position. On examining Tables 13 and 15, it is clear that primary dealers are more actively involved in the thirty-year auction than in the five-year auction. If collusion is in evidence, then price fixing effects should be more apparent in thirty-year auctions than in five-year auctions. The auction tail was defined earlier as the degree of dispersion of opinion about the value of the security. Therefore, if collusion were being practiced, one would expect smaller tails on thirty-year auctions suggesting that the dealers had conspired on pricing. An examination of the mean tails and standard deviations reveals the *reverse*. This information tends to refute the primary dealer collusion thesis.

This conclusion should not be construed as an endorsement of former auction practices. Clearly, abuses were in evidence, and as of this writing, the Treasury has taken steps to improve and expand the auction process to reduce or eliminate *any* possibility for future abuse.

Threats to the Validity of the Study

Although every precaution was taken in this study to assure the accuracy and integrity of results, upon completion and evaluation of the work several cautionary notes are in order.

First, although the data covered a ten year period, since the auctions examined occurred quarterly, this produced a maximum of forty data points per security. Furthermore, when the surprise methodology was used the number of data points dropped to between seventeen and twenty-six, depending upon the specific variable and auction being scrutinized.

Second, although many of the regressions undertaken in this study showed reasonably moderate R^2s, particularly with respect to the surprise methodology, much of the relationship between independent and dependent variables remained unexplained. It is clear that information *other than* Treasury auction results influences

market action. However, it was bey determine the nature of these other

Third, this study found mode different efficiency characteristics b thirty-year bond sectors of the U.S finding was not the focus of the stu before definitive conclusions can be 1

Fourth, this study found some 1 *of collusion* on the part of primary de research question was not the focus needs to be done to confirm this findi

Future Rese

As this study was being conducted future research became apparent.

First, given the results obtained variables which were identified but not 1 the dependent variable. Possible sugg Percent Accepted at the High Yield varial

Second, variables identified herein multiple regression in an attempt to bett between the independent and dependent

Third, new variables unrelated t researched in this study could be used in R^2 coefficients discovered in this researc include the size of primary dealer positions an institutional market sentiment indicator.

Fourth, given the interesting market e a study of other sectors of the U.S. Treast useful in determining at what point on th efficiency begins to diminish.

Fifth, given the much discussed top primary dealers, additional work needs to b indeed this practice occurs. The U.S. Trea recently taken steps to assure that the practic the future; however, there is still much debat the past.

F
York D
This stu
the thi
interest
respect

promis
prove
directic

RECENT EVENTS

As mentioned earlier in the preface to this work, several notable fixed income market events have occurred since this study was originally concluded in late 1991. This chapter is devoted in it's entirety to a thorough discussion of these recent critical events.

The *four* independent but inter-related events which will be discussed include:

1) the Salomon Brothers bidding scandal,
2) potential primary dealer collusion,
3) recent experiments in U.S. Treasury auction techniques and
4) other major Treasury market and auction reforms.

Salomon Brothers Bidding Scandal

Although some market reform mentality was gaining momentum by 1991, the incident which clearly precipitated the majority of the activity over the past two years was the Salomon Brothers bidding scandal. With the benefit of hindsight as well as completed regulatory and legal proceedings, it has now been confirmed that Salomon Brothers attempted to "corner" the market for several different U.S. Treasury securities in five different auctions beginning in December, 1990. In all cases Salomon admitted it placed *unauthorized customer bids* in the following U.S. Treasury auctions:

1) December 27, 1990 four year note,
2) February 7, 1991 30 year bond,
3) February 21, 1991 five year note,
4) April 25, 1991 five year note and
5) May 22, 1991 two year note (Department of the Treasury 1992, C1-C5).

Although the specific details of each of the above incidents were somewhat different, the common theme was the attempt by Salomon in each instance to circumvent the Treasury's 35 percent rule. As previously mentioned in Chapter two this rule precludes a single bidder from purchasing more than 35 percent of any issue being auctioned. Essentially by combining their own bids of nearly 35 percent with several unauthorized customer bids of large size, Salomon achieved effective control of several of the above auctions.

The February 1991 five year note initially attracted the scrutiny of the Treasury due to uncertainty as to the exact name of the customer for whom Salomon was purportedly bidding. At that time this particular controversy was defused as Salomon offered an acceptable explanation to the Treasury.

The occurrence which generally is credited with triggering the confluence of events which ultimately led to the legal and regulatory proceedings against Salomon was the May 1991 two year note auction. After completion of this particular auction a "short squeeze" developed in the two year note because Salomon and several customers (via largely *authorized* bids in this case) managed to purchase and control *94 percent* of the auction total. A short squeeze occurs when short sellers find themselves unable to locate the specific security which they are short in the marketplace. They are then forced to purchase or borrow the securities in order to redeliver them to those controlling the issue thus driving the price up even higher and increasing the profits to the controlling group (Department of the Treasury 1992, C5).

This "squeeze" prompted regulators to investigate Salomon's purchases of the two year notes. On May 29, the Treasury staff notified the SEC that a "squeeze" was in evidence with respect to the two year note and also of complaints from various other market participants. The "squeeze" also attracted Congressional interest.

After several months of meetings between the officials of Salomon Brothers, the Treasury, Federal Reserve, SEC and Justice

Department, the Treasury announced on August 18th that Salomon, until further notice, would no longer be allowed to enter bids in subsequent auctions for customer accounts. They would retain the right to enter bids for their own account while the investigation proceeded.

This announcement was followed later in the same month by the resignation of Salomon Brothers Chairman John Gutfreund and President Thomas Strauss. This action was deemed necessary by regulators because it was determined that both parties were aware of the wrongdoing and did nothing to prevent it.

Following the resignation pronouncements, Salomon declared Warren Buffett the new Chairman of the Board. Buffett is a well known and regarded investment professional who owned a sizable portion of Salomon Brothers stock.

During the intervening months more details regarding the wrongdoing were exposed. Paul Mozer, Salomon Brother's former chief government bond trader, became a party of particular interest to regulators since he was believed to be the individual most tightly linked to the scandal. He was released from the firm shortly after the scandal became public.

By May of 1992, the investigation had progressed to the point where Mr. Buffett deemed it necessary to attempt to settle the matter out of court as expeditiously as possible. In light of that decision, the SEC and other government agencies announced a settlement agreement with Salomon Brothers. Under the terms, Salomon paid $290 million to regulators; $190 million in fines and $100 million to a fund to repay those injured by their actions. Also pursuant to the agreement, Salomon neither admitted nor denied any wrongdoing in the matter and most importantly (from their perspective) received assurance that no criminal charges would be filed against them. Finally in a separate but related announcement, the Federal Reserve Bank of New York declared it's intention to retain Salomon Brothers as a primary dealer (Siconolfi, May 21, 1992, A1).

As for Paul Mozer, the SEC has filed various indictments against him for his personal role in the affair. Following the collapse of an earlier plea agreement, federal prosecutors as of this writing, are pursuing an indictment consisting of four felony counts. These include one count of securities fraud, two counts of making false statements and one count of preparing false books and statements. Given the nature of these new accusations, some legal experts believe a prison sentence to be quite likely if Mozer is convicted.

Potential Primary Dealer Collusion

When the Salomon Brothers incidents were initially announced in May of 1991 some media and Congressional interest again arose in the possibility of primary government dealer collusion as the source of the "squeeze". In the investigation which ensued this important issue was thoroughly explored.

The results of this inquiry failed to prove the existence of any *primary dealer collusion*. Under the terms of Salomon's plea they admitted no wrongdoing and no co-conspirators were named, therefore as of this writing the *exact* sequence of events is still unclear. Although no additional indictments have been filed, a grand jury is examining the relationship which existed between Salomon Brothers and *three customers*: Steinhardt Partners, Quantum Fund and Tiger Management (Connor, September 16, 1992, C1).

These three customers are generally known as "hedge funds". For purposes of this study a "hedge fund" shall be defined as a *private investment partnership which engages in active trading and arbitrage* (Department of the Treasury 1992, B64). In this particular case their trading focus was the government securities market.

Publicly available data on hedge funds is somewhat limited as they are largely exempt from most regulatory oversight. For example, no SEC jurisdiction is appropriate since the funds are typically privately offered, thus no offering document is filed with the SEC. They also escape scrutiny as securities dealers since they typically claim an exclusion from the Securities Exchange Act of 1934 under Section 15(a). This allows "traders" who do not transact public securities business but instead only trade for their own account to be exempt from the reporting and oversight requirements of securities dealers. They can typically be structured to avoid registration as an investment company under the Investment Company Act of 1940 as well since they usually have fewer than 100 investors and do not intend to make a public offering in the future. Finally, hedge funds are typically also exempt from the jurisdiction of the Investment Advisors Act of 1940. In this case an exemption from registration exists if the advisor has fewer than 15 clients. In 1985 the SEC adopted Rule 203 (b)(3)-1 which permitted a general partner to count an entire limited partnership as one single client rather than the sum total of the individual investors in the limited partnership (Department of the Treasury 1992, B66-B68).

The only regulatory agency which has any degree of contact or control over the typical hedge fund is the Commodity Futures Trading Commission (CFTC) since most hedge funds utilize futures contracts for trading and hedging purposes. Under the Commodity Exchange Act (CEA), registration of hedge funds is not specifically required, however registration of the hedge fund manager and advisor is required under certain circumstances. This registration requirement involves providing the CFTC with disclosure documents and certified annual reports to investors. Additionally, information must be maintained which includes records of commodity and cash market trading activity and information concerning the investment pools which are being managed (Department of the Treasury 1992, B68).

Given the unavailability of information, as mentioned above a grand jury was impaneled in September, 1992 for the express purpose of exploring the precise relationship between the three hedge funds and Salomon Brothers. Specifically, the investigation centers on the April and May 1991 auctions of the five year and two year note respectively. Those familiar with the probe estimate the inquiry will require a minimum of one year. As of this writing no further information on this matter has been made public.

Since this particular recent event is still developing, definitive statements of resolution on this subject cannot be made. However, it would appear, based upon grand jury subpoenas that the inquiry in process is largely directed toward the relationship which existed between Salomon and the three hedge funds. At this juncture, *if collusion existed*, it appears more likely to have occurred between Salomon and several customers rather than two or more primary dealers. This subjective finding confirms this author's analytical findings mentioned earlier in Chapter four.

Other recent research conducted by Vincent Reinhart in 1992 also tends to confirm this finding. In his work he reached the conclusion that "cornering" any specific market is more likely to be the work of *one aggressive single dealer* rather than a joint conspiracy of several dealers. His rational is based upon the fact that there exists a great deal of mistrust amongst primary dealers and the current auction format is unlikely to forge any new alliances. The fact that primary dealers also execute business through interdealer brokers also confirms the existence of mistrust since these interdealer brokers provide anonymity to both parties on each side of a given transaction (Reinhart 1992, 409).

Recent Experiments in U.S. Treasury Auction Techniques

As initially mentioned in Chapter two, several prominent economists for many years have contended that the auction process is inherently flawed and in need of dramatic revision or modification. The admissions and pronouncements discussed above only served to intensify these beliefs and to strengthen the rational for some alternate approach.

The standard of auction taxonomy was originally developed by William Vickrey in 1961. He developed a set of consistent and logical auction classifications which still represent the universe of generally accepted auction choices. In some cases market terminology is not compatible with Vickrey's taxonomy and when such is the case it will be noted.

The *multiple-price, sealed-bid* is the auction procedure which is currently in use for Treasury auctions. The financial community refers to this as an English auction. In any case bidders express their bidding intentions on tender forms which are turned in prior to a predetermined time. The auctioneer then ranks the bids submitted by all bidders from highest tendered price to lowest and makes awards at the highest prices which cover the total auction size. Thus participants pay differing prices depending upon the price they individually bid and the surest winner is the bidder who bids furthest above the market consensus. This results in the "winners curse" as described earlier in Chapter two. Those critical of this auction process contend that the risk of the "winners curse" puts a large premium on market information as the auction deadline approaches and enlarges the possibility of collusive or other illegal behavior (Chari & Weber 1992, 3).

The *descending-price, open outcry* auction is a procedure where bidders congregate in a single room (or the electronic equivalent) with an auctioneer calling out a sequence of decreasing prices. Using government securities as the auction item would imply an eager bidder obtaining the security at a relatively high price with the auction continuing and subsequent bidders buying at successively lower prices. The strategic decision related to bidding strategy is identical to that encountered with the above mentioned multiple-price, sealed-bid auction ie. the bidder wants to avoid being overly aggressive and purchasing the securities at a relatively high price thus incurring the dreaded "winners curse." As a result, investors have the same incentive to pool information mentioned above (Reinhart 1992, 405).

In a *ascending-price, open-outcry* auction the logistics would conform precisely to the descending-price, open-outcry auction described immediately above. In this case the auctioneer calls out a succession of prices which are systematically *raised* with each new bidding round. At each price the auctioneer totals all bids and continues raising the price until the volume demanded is less than the supply being offered for sale. When that point is reached the auctioneer will know that the price previously called was the highest price consistent with selling the entire issue. In other words, the second highest price clears the market of supply. Therefore, the securities are awarded to all bidders who bid in the last round at the highest price. A fractional allocation system would necessarily have to be devised to make partial awards to those bidders who bid in the next to last round of bidding at the second highest price. From an investors perspective this auction approach lessens the chances of the "winners curse" but does not eliminate it (Reinhart 1992, 405).

The fourth and final auction type is the *uniform-price, sealed-bid*. In this type of auction the auctioneer collects sealed bids, arranges them by price and makes awards at the *single price* that exactly places the entire market supply. This is also referred to as a "second price" auction or "Dutch" auction, in the financial press. Procedurally, bidders at the highest price would receive all securities for which they bid, at the second highest price. Any excess of supply over demand at the highest price would be satisfied again according to some fractional allocation system as mentioned above. Those remaining securities would also be sold at the second highest price (Chari & Weber 1992, 3).

This fourth auction process is the approach which has gained the most favor in recent years from such eminent sources as Milton Friedman (as discussed in Chapter two) and Merton Miller

(Henriques 1991, F13). Even this alternative is not without critics however. Michael Basham for example contends that all the discussion on auction flaws and various alternatives misses the critical point that more and more investors simply ignore the entire auction process entirely and instead purchase the desired securities in advance of the actual auction through pre-auction or when-issued trading (Basham 1992, A12).

Criticism aside, due to intense public scrutiny, media attention and Congressional inquiry the Treasury did announce a one year experiment with the "Dutch" auction to commence in September 1992. Specifically the "Dutch" auction procedure was to be utilized on the twelve monthly sales of the two and five year notes over the ensuing year. The Treasury was hopeful that the experiment would result in lowering the cost of government borrowing while also thwarting any type of potential future controversial activity since it should eliminate the "winners curse" (Salwen 1992, C1).

On August 4, 1993 after awaiting the results of the above Treasury experiment in the use of the "Dutch" auction, market participants learned that the Treasury extended it's original experiment for an additional year (Vogel & Connor 1993, C21). The Treasury mentioned that the results of the experiment to date had been inconclusive and more observations on the technique would be necessary before making a final decision. The spokesperson further mentioned that the Treasury was prepared to drop the experiment if it failed to meet expectations and conversely was also prepared to institute the process permanently if results deemed it necessary. Other private sources indicate that the results on the two year note have been favorable from the Treasury's perspective (ie. lowering borrowing costs) however the five year notes have been deemed equally unfavorable (Vogel 1993, C1). The Treasury Borrowing Advisory Committee of the Public Securities Association recently released the results of research it had conducted wherein they determined the new "Dutch" auctions were responsible for lower post-auction volatility (Connor August 27 1993, A5A). A final decision should be expected on this matter in August of 1994.

Other Major Market and Auction Reforms

As mentioned earlier in this chapter, the Salomon Brothers scandal provided a triggering mechanism which set off a chain of events much more far reaching than those already described above. Once the magnitude and severity of the violations became apparent to regulators and Congressional interests, a tidal wave of reforms began to sweep Washington. These reforms were summarized concisely in the *Joint Report on the Securities Market* and can be classified as either: 1) administrative or regulatory in nature or 2) legislative, thus requiring congressional legal action.

The administrative and regulatory changes can be categorized into five areas:

1) Broadening participation in auctions,
2) Stronger enforcement of auction rules,
3) Detecting and combatting short squeezes,
4) Changes to Treasury auction policies and
5) Improvement to the primary dealer system

In terms of broadening participation in auctions, the Treasury announced that *all* securities broker dealers could henceforth submit bids for customers in Treasury auctions. Previously only primary dealers were allowed to submit such bids. Additionally, *any bidder* with an "autocharge agreement" would be allowed to bid at auction. This privilege was also previously strictly confined to primary dealers. Finally to broaden bidding participation by small investors the noncompetitive bidding limit was raised from $1 million to $5 million.

As for stronger enforcement of auction rules the Federal Reserve has begun spot checking customer bids for authenticity. They also obtain specific verbal and written confirmation from any customers who receive large awards in excess of $500 million. Finally due largely to *suspected abuses* at Cantor Fitzgerald and the Chicago Corporation relating to noncompetitive bidding practices, the rules have also been tightened substantially on these bids as well (Connor September 7 1993, A16).

In detecting and combatting short squeezes, the Treasury announced that it will provide the market with additional supply of any security that is the subject of an acute protracted shortage *without evidence* of manipulation as a necessity (Salwen 1992, C1). Further a new working group of Agency participants was formed to work together in improving market surveillance.

The major changes to Treasury auction policies included an acceleration in the movement toward an automated auction system. As of May, 1993 this system was fully functional with 37 of 39 primary dealers signed on and a total of 280 competitive bids received in the May thirty year bond auction. This system has dramatically hastened the turnaround time for receipt of auction results from several hours a number of years ago to nine minutes at this particular auction (Connor May 24 1993, A5C). Once the above system has received thorough testing under rigorous conditions, the Treasury may consider implementing an open method of auctioning securities as described in detail above (either ascending or descending price; open outcry).

The final administrative reforms undertaken involved improvement in the primary dealer system. One approach opened up the system to more potential primary dealers by eliminating the requirement that each dealer must consistently maintain a one percent share of customer trades in the secondary market. Primary dealers would still be required to maintain adequate capital standards and must maintain reasonably good secondary markets. Finally, the issue of direct regulatory authority was placed squarely on the SEC, not the Federal Reserve Bank of New York as many had been led to believe.

Legislative actions as mentioned above obviously require congressional action and therefore can be viewed only as recommendations. One of the strongest recommendations emanating from the *Joint Report* was the reauthorization of Treasury rulemaking authority under the Government Securities Act (GSA) of 1986. Under this legislation previous gaps and loopholes in then existing statutes were closed and stricter surveillance and enforcement of regulation was promoted. When the Salomon Brothers scandal erupted in 1991 Congress was debating the extension of GSA which was to expire on October 1, 1991. Because of the furor over the Salomon incident, a consensus could not be reached and as a result the law expired and has never been reinstated.

Another legislative recommendation included making misleading written statements to an issuer of government securities an explicit violation of the Securities Act of 1934 with appropriate penalties.

A proposed rule on backup position reporting would allow the Treasury to request reports from holders of large positions of specific government securities. This proposal would presumably alleviate the "squeeze" problem mentioned above as dealers would be forced to open their books directly to regulators. This option is supported by the Treasury, SEC and Federal Reserve Bank of New York and was recently recommended by the House Energy and Commerce Committee as part of their compromise bill.

Other proposals such as imposing sales practice rules, requiring an annual SEC report on the adequacy of bond price dissemination and requiring time sequenced audit trails were also recommended by the House committee . As of this writing the compromise measure must still pass the full House and be reconciled with an earlier

Senate version but passage appears likely (Connor September 15 1993, A14).

Conclusion

The market for U.S. Treasury securities is vast and complex. With nearly $4 trillion dollars of outstanding debt, a single basis point increase in the financing cost on the government debt costs the taxpayer in *excess of $300 million each year*. Given the enormity of these costs it is imperative that an effective and efficient financing mechanism for the U.S. government debt be established and maintained.

Although problems have occurred recently in the marketplace as described herein, it is important to note that the system is *not completely broken* but instead is only in need of *repair*. Our financing techniques, even though somewhat flawed, are still the envy of most of our trading partners around the world. Therefore dramatic or draconian changes in the system should be considered only as a last resort and certainly future changes of *any type* should be undertaken only after extensive analysis indicates that no irreparable damage will be inflicted upon the marketplace.

BIBLIOGRAPHY

Barro, Robert J. (1986). Futures markets and the fluctuations in inflation, monetary growth and asset returns. *Journal of Business*, 59(2), 21-38.

Basham, Michael E. (1992, July 23). The dutch auction, abogus solution. *The Wall Street Journal*. A12.

Bierwag, G. O., Kaufman, George G., & Latta, Cynthia. (1987). Bond portfolio immunization: tests of maturity, one and two factor duration matching strategies. *Financial Review*, 22(2), 203-19.

Blustein, Paul (1990, November 11). Slow pace in Tokyo trading room: slackening participation in Treasury auctions may pose serious problem for U. S. economy. *Washington Post*, pp. H1, H6.

Board of Governors of the Federal Reserve System. (1984). *The Federal Reserve System: purposes and functions*. (7th ed.). Washington, D.C.: Publications Services.

Boatler, Robert. (1985). Determinants of Treasury bill auction spreads: an update with evidence of market learning to cope with instability. *Quarterly Journal of Business & Economics*, 24(1), 36-42.

Bolten, Steven. (1973). Treasury bill auction procedures: an empirical investigation. *Journal of Finance*, June, 577-584.

Bowles, David, Ulbrick, Holley, and Wallace, Myles. (1989). Default risk, interest differentials and fiscal policy: a new look at crowding out. *Eastern Economic Journal*, 15(3), 203-12.

Brennan, William. (1989, October). Buying treasuries direct. *Small Business Reports*, pp 76-77.

Brigham, Eugene (1989). *Fundamentals of financial management* (5th ed.). Chicago: The Dryden Press.

Brigham, Eugene F. & Gapenski, Louis C. (1988). *Financial management: theory and practice* (5th ed.). Chicago: The Dryden Press.

Brigham, Eugene F. & Gapenski, Louis C. (1990). *Intermediate financial management* (3rd ed.). Chicago: The Dryden Press.

Bronfenbrenner, Martin & Sichel, Werner & Gardner, Wayland. (1990). *Macroeconomics* (3rd ed.). Dallas: Houghton Mifflin.

Byrkit, Donald R. (1979). *Business Statistics*. New York: D. Van Nostrand Company.

Byrns, Ralph & Stone, Gerald. (1989). *Macroeconomics* (4th ed.). Glenview: Scott Foresman.

Byrns, Ralph & Stone, Gerald. (1989). *Microeconomics* (4th ed.). Glenview: Scott Foresman.

Calvo, Guillermo A. (1988). Servicing the public debt: the role of expectations. *American Economic Review, 78*(4), 647-661.

Cammack, Elizabeth B. (1987). Evidence of bidding strategies and the information contained in Treasury bill auctions (Doctoral dissertation, University of Chicago, 1987). *Dissertations Abstracts International, 48*, 188.

Campbell, John. (1986). A defense of the traditional hypothesis about the term structure of interest rates. *Journal of Finance, 41*(1), 183-93.

Campbell, John & Shiller, Robert J. (1989). Yield spreads and interest rate movements. *NBER Working Paper, 3153*. (From *CFA Digest*, 1989/1990, *20* (1))

Cargill, Thomas F. (1991). *Money, the financial system and monetary policy* (4th. ed.). Englewood Cliffs: Prentice Hall.

Cebula, Richard J., Carlos, Chistopher & Koch, James V. (1981). The "crowding out" effect of federal government outlay decisions: an empirical note. *Public Choice*, 92, 329-336.

Chance, Don M. (1989). *Options and futures*. Chicago: Dryden.

Chari, V.V. & Weber, Robert J. (1992). How the Treasury should auction its debt. *Federal Reserve Bank of Minneapolis*, Fall, 3-11.

Christofides, L.N. (1980). An empirical analysis of bond markets and their implications for the term structure of interest rates. *Manchester School of Economics and Social Studies*, *48*(2), 111-25.

Cohen, Laurie P. & Salwen Kevin G. (1991, September 16). Treasuries market inquiry widens; Steinhardt comes under scrutiny. *The Wall Street Journal*. p.C1.

Cohen, Laurie P. & Siconolfi, Michael. (1991, September 5). Salomon reveals it had control of 94 percent of notes at May auction: more shadows cast on Wall Street firms. *The Wall Street Journal*. pp. C1, C14.

Cohen, Laurie P. & Siconolfi, Michael. (1991, October 7). Before May's squeeze, one in April wounded investors in Treasuries. *The Wall Street Journal*. p. A10.

Cohen, Laurie P., Siconolfi, Michael & Salwen, Kevin G. (1991, August 21). Firms review their treasury operations. *The Wall Street Journal*. pp. C1, C12.

Cohen, Laurie P., Siconolfi, Michael & Salwen, Kevin G. (1991, August 27). SEC probes collusion by traders. *The Wall Street Journal*. pp C1,C16.

Connor, John. (1993, September 15). Bill to regulate Treasury market passes house panel. *The Wall Street Journal*. A14.

Connor, John. (1993, May 24). Treasury's automated auction system working well despite earlier concerns. *The Wall Street Journal*. A5C.

Connor, John. (1993, August 27). Single price securities experiment by U.S. finds method curbs volatility. *The Wall Street Journal*. A5A.

Connor, John. (1993, September 7). SEC tries to settle with Chicago Corp., Cantor Fitzgerald on Treasury bidding. *The Wall Street Journal*. A16.

Conner, John & Salwen, Kevin. (1992, September 16). Grand jury set to study sales of U.S. notes. *The Wall Street Journal*. p.C6.

Cooper, S. K. & Fraser, Donald (1987). *The financial marketplace* (2nd ed.). Reading, Massachusetts: Addison - Wesley.

Council of Economic Advisors. (1991). *Economic Report of the President* (Superintendent of Documents # PR 41.9:1991). Washington D.C.: U.S. Government Printing Office.

Cox, Michael (1985). The behavior of Treasury securities monthly 1942-1984. *Journal of Monetary Economics*, September, 227-250.

Darrat, Ali F. (1990). Structural federal deficits and interest rates: some casualty and co-integration tests. *Southern Economic Journal*, 56(3), 752-59.

Department of the Treasury, Securities and Exchange Commission &
    Board of Governors of the Federal Reserve System. (1992).
    Joint report on the government securities market (ISBN No. 0-
    16-036093-5). Washington, DC: U.S. Government Printing
    Office.

Elliott, J.W. & Echols, M.E. (1976). Market segmentation; speculative
    behavior and the term structure of interest rates. *Review of
    Economics and Statistics, 63*(1), 40-47.

Engelbrecht-Wiggans, Richard. (1980). Auction and bidding models:
    a survey. *Management Science, 26*(2), 119-142.

Erbas, Nuri S. (1989). The limits on bond financing of government
    deficits under optimal fiscal policy. *Journal of
    Macroeconomics, 11*(4), 589-98.

Evans, Paul. (1985). Do large deficits produce high interest rates?
    American Economic Review, 75(1), 68-87.

Fabozzi, T., Tong, Tom & Zhu, Yu. (1990). Symmetric cash
    matching. *Financial Analysts Journal, 46*(5), 47.

Fair, Ray C. (1988). Optimal choice of monetary policy. *Economics,
    22*(2), 301-15.

Fama, Eugene F. (1990). Term structure forecasts of interest rates,
    inflation and real returns. *Journal of Monetary Economics,
    25*(1), 59-76.

First Boston Corporation. (1981). *Fixed income glossary: common
    bond market terminology*. New York: First Boston.

First Boston Corporation. (1990). *The Handbook of Securities of the
    United States Government and Federal Agencies* (34th ed.).
    New York: First Boston.

Fischer, Donald E. & Jordan, Ronald J. (1991). *Security analysis and portfolio management* (5th ed.). Englewood Cliffs: Prentice Hall.

Fong, Gifford H. (1990). Portfolio construction: fixed income. In J.L. Maginn & D.L. Tuttle (Eds), *Managing Investment Portfolios: A Dynamic Process* (pp. 52-53). Boston: Warren, Gorham & Lamont.

Fraser, Donald R. (1977). On the accuracy and usefulness of interest rate forecasts. *Business Economics, 12*(4), 38-44.

Friedman, Benjamin. (1990). Changing effects of monetary policy on real economic activity. *NBER working paper, 3278*. (From *CFA Digest*, 1990, *20* (3))

Friedman, Milton. (1963). Price determination in the U.S. Treasury bill market: a comment. *Review of Economics and Statistics, 45*, 318-320.

Friedman, Milton. (1991, August 28). How to sell government securities. *The Wall Street Journal,* p. A10.

Gemmell, Norman. (1988). Debt servicing costs and the growth of public expenditures. *Public Finance, 43*(2), 223-35.

Gilpin, Kenneth. (1990, October 10). Prices of Treasury issues plunge: budget agreement viewed negatively. *The New York Times*, p. 12.

Gitman, Lawrence & Joehnk, Michael. (1990). *Personal financial planning* (5th ed.). Chicago: Dryden.

Grieves, Robin & Marcus, Alan J. (1990). Riding the yield curve. *NBER working paper, 3511*. (From *CFA Digest*, 1990/1991, *21* (1))

Harris, Milton & Raviv, Arthur. (1981). Allocation mechanisms and the design of auctions. *Econometrica, 49*(6), 1477-1499.

Havrilesky, Thomas M. & Boorman, John T. (1982). *Money supply, money demand and macroeconomic models* (2nd. ed.). Arlington Heights: Harlan Davidson.

Henriques, Diana B. (1991, September 15). Treasury's troubled auctions. *The New York Times*. F13.

Herman, Tom. (1987, July 30). Bond prices rally sparked by reports congress will fortify Gramm Rudman. *The Wall Street Journal*, pp. 32,37.

Heyne, Paul (1991). *The Economic way of thinking* (6th. ed.). New York: Macmillan.

Hoelscher, Gregory. (1986). New evidence on deficits and interest rates. *Journal of Money, Credit and Banking, 18*(1), 1-17.

Homer, Sidney & Liebowitz, Martin. (1972). *Inside the yield book*. Englewood Cliffs: Prentice Hall.

Ibbotson, Roger & Sinquefield, Rex. (1989). *Stocks, bonds, bills and inflation: historical returns* (1926-1987). Chicago: Dow Jones - Irwin.

Kahn, George. (1990). The changing interest sensitivity of the U.S. economy. *Economic Review of the Federal Reserve Bank of Kansas City, 74*(9), 13-34. (From *CFA Digest*, 1989/1990, *20*(3))

Kaufman, George G. (1989). *The U.S. financial system: money, markets and institutions*. Englewood Cliffs: Prentice Hall.

Keynes, John Maynard. (1935). *The General theory of employment, interest and money.* New York: Harcourt, Brace.

Kiem, Donald & Stambaugh, Robert. (1986). Predicting returns in the stock and bond markets. *Journal of Financial Economics, 17*, 357-390.

Langetieg, Terence C., Liebowitz, Martin L. & Kogelman, Stanley. (1990). Duration targeting and the management of multi-period returns. *Financial Analysts Journal, 46*(5), 35-42.

Levine, Sumner (Ed.). (1975). *Financial analysts handbook: portfolio management*. Homewood: Dow Jones.

Livingston, Miles. (1981). Taxation and bond market equilibrium in a world of uncertain interest rates: a reply. *Journal of Financial & Quantitative Analysis, 16*(5), 779-81.

Mankiw, Gregory. (1986). The term structure of interest rates revisited. *Brookings Papers on Economic Activity*, 61-96.

Marcial, Gene. (1985, February 4). First Boston's bungled bid. *Business Week* p. 76.

Markowitz, Harry. (1959). *Portfolio selection and efficient diversification of investments*. New York: John Wiley and sons.

Marsh, Terry & Rosenfeld, Eric. (1983). Stochastic processes for interest rates and equilibrium bond prices. *Journal of Finance, 38*(2), 635-46.

Mason, Robert D. & Lind, Douglas A. (1990). *Statistical techniques in business and economics* (7th ed.). Homewood: Irwin.

McCallum, Bennett. (1984). Are bond financed deficits inflationary: a Ricardian analysis. *Journal of Political Economy, 92*, 123-135.

McConnell, Campbell. (1987). *Economics* (10th ed.). New York: McGraw-Hill.

Meltzer, Allan H. (1984). The case for a monetary rule. In T. M. Havrilesky (Ed.), *Modern Concepts in Macroeconomics* (pp. 445-448). Arlington Heights: Harlan Davidson.

Miller, Merton. (1977). Debt and taxes. *Journal of Finance, 32*(2), 261-275.

Miller, Roger L. & Pulsinelli, Robert W. (1985). *Modern money and banking.* New York: Mc-Graw Hill.

Modigliani, Franco & Sutch, Richard. (1966). Innovations in interest rate policy. *American Economic Review, 61*(2), 178-197.

Moses, Johnathan M. (1993,January 13). Prosecutors file broader charges against Mozer. *The Wall Street Journal.* p.C1.

Mulligan, James G. (1989). *Managerial economics: strategy for profit.* Boston: Allyn & Bacon.

Parkin, Michael. (1990). *Economics.* Reading, Mass.: Addison-Wesley.

Pesando, James E. (1981). On forecasting interest rates: an efficient markets perspective. *Journal of Monetary Economics, 8*, 305-318.

Pesando, James E. & Plourde, Andre. (1988). The October 1979 change in U.S. monetary regime: it's impact on the forecastability of Canadian interest rates. *Journal of Finance, 43*(1), 217-39.

Peterson, Willis. (1989). *Macro* (7th ed.). Homewood: Irwin.

Prell, Michael. (1973). How well do the experts forecast interest rates? *Federal Reserve Bank of Kansas City,* September-October, 3-13

Reinhardt, Vincent. (1992). *An analysis of potential Treasury auction techniques* (Federal Reserve Bulletin, June). Washington, DC: U.S. Government Printing Office.

Rieber, Michael. (1965). Some characteristics of Treasury bill dealers in the auction market. *Journal of Finance*, 49-58.

Roberds, William. (1990). Money and the economy: puzzles from the 1980s experience. *Economic Review: Federal Reserve Bank of Atlanta, 74*(5), 20-35. (From *CFA Digest,* 1989/1990, *20*(2))

Robinson, William D. (1984). Government bonds and· unstable growth paths. *Quarterly Journal of Business & Economics, 23*(3), 36-58.

Rohlf, William D. Jr. (1989). *Economic reasoning.* Reading: Addison-Wesley.

Salwen, Kevin G. & Wessel, David. (1991, September 9). U.S. hastens to alter its debt sales. *The Wall Street Journal,* pp. C1, C11.

Salwen, Kevin G. (1992, January 20). Agencies to combat squeezes. *The Wall Street Journal.* C1 & C13.

Salwen, Kevin G. & Connor, John. (1992, September 4). Treasury to try "dutch" system at its auctions. *The Wall Street Journal.* pp. C1 & C15.

Schafer, Stephen. (1981). Taxation and bond market equilibrium in a world of uncertain interest rates: a comment. *Journal of Financial & Quantitative Analysis, 16*(5), 773-77.

Schirm, David, Sheehan, Richard, & Ferri, Michael. (1989). Financial market responses to Treasury debt announcements: a note. *Journal of Money, Credit & Banking, 21*(3), 394-400.

Scott, James, & Wolf, Charles. (1979). The efficient diversification of bids in Treasury bill auctions. *Review of Economics & Statistics, 61*(2), 280-287.

Screpanti, Ernesto. (1989) Monetary dynamics, speculation and the term structure of interest rates. *Economic Notes, 2,* 167-91.

Sharpe, William. (1964). Capital asset prices: a theory of market equilibrium under conditions of risk. *Journal of Finance, 19,* 425-442.

Siconolfi, Michael & Sesit, Michael R. & Mitchell, Constance. (1991, August 19). Collusion, price fixing have long been rife in the Treasury market. *The Wall Street Journal*, pp. A1, A5.

Siconolfi, Michael & Cohen, Laurie & Salwen, Kevin. (1992, May 21). Salomon is breathing easier after accepting huge fine in scandal. *The Wall Street Journal*. p.A6.

Sivesind, Charles. (1978, Autumn). Non competitive tenders in Treasury auctions: how much do they affect savings flows. *Federal Reserve Bank of New York Quarterly Review, 3*(3), pp. 34-38.

Smith, Vernon. (1966). Bidding theory and the Treasury bill auction: does price discrimination increase bill prices? *Review of Economics and Statistics*, May, 141-146.

Streifford, David M. (1990). *Economic perspective*. Homewood: Irwin.

Swamy, Paravastu & Kolluri, Baharat. (1990), What do regressions of interest rates on deficits imply? *Southern Economic Journal, 56*(4), 1010-28.

Thomas, Lloyd B. Jr, & Abderrazak, Ali. (1988). Anticipated future budget deficits and the term structure of interest rates. *Southern Economic Journal, 55*(1), 150-161.

Thomas, Paulette & Herman, Tom (1991, October 28). Treasury sets bidding rules aimed at cleaning up troubled auctions. *The Wall Street Journal*, pp.C1, C16.

U.S. Bureau of the Census, *Statistical Abstract of the United States: 1986*. (106th edition). Washington, D.C., 1986.

U.S. Bureau of the Census, *Statistical Abstract of the United States: 1990*. (110th edition). Washington, D.C., 1990.

Valentine, Jerome L. & Mennis, Edmund. (1971). *Quantitative techniques for financial analysis*. Homewood: Irwin.

Vickrey, William. (1961). Counterspeculation, auctions and competitive sealed tenders. *Journal of Finance, 16*, 8-37.

Vogel, Thomas T. (1993, January 4). Dutch auctions appear to be mixed blessing for U.S. *The Wall Street Journal*. pp.C1 & C17.

Vogel, Thomas T. & Connor, John. (1993, August 5). Treasury prices drop on news of record size of refunding, concerns about July jobs data. *The Wall Street Journal*. p. C21.

Wachtel, Paul & Young, John. (1987). Deficit announcements and interest rates. *American Economic Review, 77*, 1007-1012.

Wachtel, Paul & Young, John. (1990). The impact of Treasury auction announcements on interest rates. *Quarterly Review of Economics and Business*, Autumn, 62-72.

Wallace, David. (1985, January 21). Inside a Treasury auction: a bond trader's billion dollar day. *Business Week*, pp. 92, 93, 96.

Walsh, Carl E. (1984). Interest rate volatility and monetary policy. *Journal of Money, Credit and Banking, 16*, 133-150.

Waud, Roger N. (1989). *Microeconomics* (4th. ed.). New York: Harper & Row.

Webster, Charles E. Jr. (1983). The effects of deficits on interest rates. In D.R. Fraser & P.S. Rose (Eds.). *Financial institutions and markets in a changing world*. Plano: Business Publications, Inc.

Weil, Philippe. (1987). Permanent budget deficits and inflation. *Journal of Monetary Economics, 20*(2), 393-410.

Wessel, David & Salwen, Kevin G. (1991, September 12). U.S. acts to change auctions of Treasuries. *The Wall Street Journal*, pp. C1, C18.

Weston, Fred J. & Brigham Eugene F. (1990). *Essentials of managerial finance* (9th. ed.). Chicago: Dryden.

Weston, J. Fred & Copeland, Thomas. (1986). *Managerial finance* (8th ed.). Chicago: The Dryden Press.

Whittaker, J. Gregg. (1990). Interest rate swaps: risk and regulation. In J.A. Wilcox (Ed.) *Current readings on money, banking and financial markets*. pp 73-83. Glenview: Scott Foresman.

APPENDIX A

FIVE YEAR AUCTION RESULTS:
ALL DATA

	TABLE A-1			TABLE A-2

TABLE A-1 / TABLE A-2

FIVE YEAR AUCTIONS		FIVE YEAR AUCTIONS	
Independent variable: Coverage Ratio		Independent variable: Tail	
Regression Output:		Regression Output:	
Constant	0.02720832	Constant	-0.0601608
Std Err of Y Est	0.15057876	Std Err of Y Est	0.14458496
R Squared	0.00404498	R Squared	0.08175513
No. of Observations	40	No. of Observations	40
Degrees of Freedom	38	Degrees of Freedom	38
Computed "t"	-0.3929	Computed "t"	1.8394
X Coefficient(s)	-0.02077982	X Coefficient(s)	0.01980044
Std Err of Coef.	0.05289461	Std Err of Coef.	0.01076477

Y DAY 0/-1 BP CHG	X Coverage Ratio	Y DAY 0/-1 BP CHG	X TAIL
0.42	1.93	0.42	11
-0.31	1.88	-0.31	3
0.21	2.48	0.21	2
0.05	2.50	0.05	2
0.19	2.44	0.19	2
-0.25	1.67	-0.25	7
0.16	1.99	0.16	5
-0.56	2.54	-0.56	2
-0.05	1.99	-0.05	4
0.05	2.57	0.05	2
-0.06	2.33	-0.06	1
-0.06	2.04	-0.06	2
-0.01	1.99	-0.01	4
-0.07	2.25	-0.07	0
0.12	2.03	0.12	3
-0.10	2.97	-0.10	0
0.03	2.33	0.03	1
-0.08	2.36	-0.08	3
-0.04	2.56	-0.04	0
-0.02	2.81	-0.02	1
-0.05	2.75	-0.05	0
-0.05	2.17	-0.05	1
-0.02	3.22	-0.02	1
-0.12	3.34	-0.12	0
-0.14	2.55	-0.14	1
-0.10	2.33	-0.10	2
-0.10	2.82	-0.10	1
-0.03	3.02	-0.03	1
-0.03	3.24	-0.03	1
0.05	2.92	0.05	0
0.06	2.46	0.06	1
0.01	2.68	0.01	1
-0.01	3.04	-0.01	1
-0.01	3.50	-0.01	0
-0.02	2.97	-0.02	0
-0.02	2.90	-0.02	1
0.04	2.78	0.04	0
0.01	2.76	0.01	0
-0.12	3.35	-0.12	0
-0.03	2.93	-0.03	1

Source: Y Table 11; Column (7).
X Table 9: Column (5).

Source: Y Table 11; Column (7).
X Table 9: Column (9).

TABLE A-3

FIVE YEAR AUCTIONS	
Independent variable: NCmp %	
Regression Output:	
Constant	-0.00388574026
Std Err of Y Est	0.012450597992
R Squared	0.001311884419
No. of Observations	40
Degrees of Freedom	38
Computed "t"	0.2234
X Coefficient(s)	0.007902456247
Std Err of Coef.	0.035370195119

Y DAY 0/-1 % CHG	X NCmp %
0.031	0.101
-0.031	0.112
0.018	0.147
0.004	0.170
0.014	0.138
-0.018	0.172
0.010	0.151
-0.042	0.176
-0.004	0.148
0.004	0.183
-0.005	0.227
-0.006	0.175
-0.001	0.166
-0.007	0.184
0.010	0.221
-0.009	0.089
0.003	0.080
-0.006	0.115
-0.003	0.080
-0.002	0.071
-0.004	0.082
-0.005	0.087
-0.002	0.088
-0.013	0.109
-0.017	0.060
-0.013	0.043
-0.015	0.032
-0.004	0.031
-0.004	0.032
0.006	0.044
0.007	0.047
0.001	0.039
-0.001	0.042
-0.001	0.075
-0.002	0.083
-0.002	0.073
0.004	0.089
0.001	0.075
-0.014	0.044
-0.004	0.034

Source: Table 11; Column (7) %.

X Table 9; Column (11).

TABLE A-4	TABLE A-5

<table>
<tr><td colspan="2">FIVE YEAR AUCTIONS</td><td colspan="2">FIVE YEAR AUCTIONS</td></tr>
</table>

TABLE A-4

FIVE YEAR AUCTIONS

Independent variable: NYAcc % Ttl

Regression Output:

Constant	0.0017083
Std Err of Y Est	0.0099993
R Squared	0.0013315
No. of Observations	37
Degrees of Freedom	35
Computed "t"	-0.2160
X Coefficient(s)	-0.006252
Std Err of Coef.	0.028942

Y	X
DAY 0/-1	NYAcc
% CHG	as % Ttl
0.004	0.805
0.014	0.846
-0.018	0.718
0.010	0.804
-0.042	0.888
-0.004	0.801
0.004	0.843
-0.005	0.861
-0.006	0.900
-0.001	0.826
-0.007	0.874
0.010	0.857
-0.009	0.927
0.003	0.883
-0.006	0.859
-0.003	0.916
-0.002	0.888
-0.004	0.916
-0.005	0.822
-0.002	0.878
-0.013	0.890
-0.017	0.869
-0.013	0.916
-0.015	0.937
-0.004	0.945
-0.004	0.738
0.006	0.959
0.007	0.934
0.001	0.900
-0.001	0.922
-0.001	0.936
-0.002	0.907
-0.002	0.924
0.004	0.915
0.001	0.883
-0.014	0.957
-0.004	0.960

Source: Y Table 11; Column (7) %.

X Table 9; Column (13) .

TABLE A-5

FIVE YEAR AUCTIONS

Independent variable: NYAcc % Appl

Regression Output:

Constant	-0.005238
Std Err of Y Est	0.0100028
R Squared	0.000626
No. of Observations	37
Degrees of Freedom	35
Computed "t"	0.1481
X Coefficient(s)	0.0036032
Std Err of Coef.	0.0243347

Y	X
DAY 0/-1	NYAcc
% CHG	as % Appl
0.004	0.380
0.014	0.403
-0.018	0.560
0.010	0.490
-0.042	0.413
-0.004	0.504
0.004	0.399
-0.005	0.446
-0.006	0.531
-0.001	0.496
-0.007	0.464
0.010	0.503
-0.009	0.356
0.003	0.430
-0.006	0.418
-0.003	0.414
-0.002	0.375
-0.004	0.386
-0.005	0.448
-0.002	0.317
-0.013	0.298
-0.017	0.396
-0.013	0.438
-0.015	0.373
-0.004	0.348
-0.004	0.271
0.006	0.362
0.007	0.425
0.001	0.385
-0.001	0.338
-0.001	0.296
-0.002	0.343
-0.002	0.359
0.004	0.372
0.001	0.354
-0.014	0.309
-0.004	0.351

Source: Y Table 11; Column (7) %.

X Table 9; Column (15).

TABLE A-6   TABLE A-7

FIVE YEAR AUCTIONS

Independent Variable: Coverage Ratio

Regression Output:

Constant	-0.090096
Std Err of Y Est	0.1908808
R Squared	0.0023723
No. of Observations	40
Degrees of Freedom	38
Computed "t"	0.3006021
X Coefficient(s)	0.0201559
Std Err of Coef.	0.0670517

Y DAY +1/-1 BP CHG	X Coverage Ratio
0.38	1.93
-0.42	1.88
0.37	2.48
0.06	2.50
0.15	2.44
-0.25	1.67
0.02	1.99
-0.70	2.54
-0.02	1.99
0.06	2.57
-0.13	2.33
-0.05	2.04
-0.05	1.99
-0.09	2.25
0.09	2.03
-0.05	2.97
-0.03	2.33
-0.38	2.36
-0.03	2.56
0.02	2.81
0.11	2.75
-0.11	2.17
-0.07	3.22
-0.17	3.34
-0.30	2.55
0.13	2.33
-0.11	2.82
-0.04	3.02
-0.01	3.24
0.02	2.92
0.04	2.46
0.07	2.68
-0.02	3.04
0.02	3.50
0.04	2.97
0.08	2.90
0.06	2.78
-0.02	2.76
-0.12	3.35
-0.07	2.93

Source: Y Table 11; Column (8).

X Table 9; Column (5).

FIVE YEAR AUCTIONS

Independent Variable: Tail

Regression Output:

Constant	-0.05745
Std Err of Y Est	0.1894747
R Squared	0.0170155
No. of Observations	40
Degrees of Freedom	38
Computed "t"	0.8110361
X Coefficient(s)	0.0114412
Std Err of Coef.	0.0141069

Y DAY +1/-1 BP CHG	X TAIL
0.38	11
-0.42	3
0.37	2
0.06	2
0.15	2
-0.25	7
0.02	5
-0.70	2
-0.02	4
0.06	2
-0.13	1
-0.05	2
-0.05	4
-0.09	0
0.09	3
-0.05	0
-0.03	1
-0.38	3
-0.03	0
0.02	1
0.11	0
-0.11	1
-0.07	1
-0.17	0
-0.30	1
0.13	2
-0.11	1
-0.04	1
-0.01	1
0.02	0
0.04	1
0.07	1
-0.02	1
0.02	0
0.04	0
0.08	1
0.06	0
-0.02	0
-0.12	0
-0.07	1

Source: Y Table 11; Column (8).

X Table 9; Column (9).

TABLE A-8

FIVE YEAR AUCTIONS	
Independent Variable: N Cmp. %	
Regression Output:	

Constant	-0.00165464413
Std Err of Y Est	0.016507261699
R Squared	0.004935997037
No. of Observations	40
Degrees of Freedom	38
Computed "t"	-0.43416392586
X Coefficient(s)	-0.02035991764
Std Err of Coef.	0.04689454013

Y DAY +1/-1 % CHG	X NCmp %
0.028	0.101
-0.042	0.112
0.032	0.147
0.004	0.170
0.011	0.138
-0.018	0.172
0.001	0.151
-0.053	0.176
-0.001	0.148
0.004	0.183
-0.010	0.227
-0.005	0.175
-0.005	0.166
-0.009	0.184
0.008	0.221
-0.004	0.089
-0.003	0.080
-0.027	0.115
-0.002	0.080
0.002	0.071
0.010	0.082
-0.011	0.087
-0.007	0.088
-0.018	0.109
-0.037	0.060
0.017	0.043
-0.017	0.032
-0.006	0.031
-0.001	0.032
0.002	0.044
0.005	0.047
0.008	0.039
-0.003	0.042
0.002	0.075
0.004	0.083
0.009	0.073
0.006	0.089
-0.002	0.075
-0.014	0.044
-0.009	0.034

Source: Y Table 11; Column (8) %.

X Table 9; Column (11).

	TABLE A-9			TABLE A-10	

TABLE A-9

FIVE YEAR AUCTIONS

Independent Variable: NY Acc % Ttl

Regression Output:

Constant	-0.023239
Std Err of Y Est	0.0137164
R Squared	0.0081041
No. of Observations	37
Degrees of Freedom	35
Computed "t"	0.5347546
X Coefficient(s)	0.0212302
Std Err of Coef.	0.0397009

Y	X
DAY +1/-1	NY Acc
% CHG	% Ttl
0.004	0.805
0.011	0.846
-0.018	0.718
0.001	0.804
-0.053	0.888
-0.001	0.801
0.004	0.843
-0.010	0.861
-0.005	0.900
-0.005	0.826
-0.009	0.874
0.008	0.857
-0.004	0.927
-0.003	0.883
-0.027	0.859
-0.002	0.916
0.002	0.888
0.010	0.916
-0.011	0.822
-0.007	0.878
-0.018	0.890
-0.037	0.869
0.017	0.916
-0.017	0.937
-0.006	0.945
-0.001	0.738
0.002	0.959
0.005	0.934
0.008	0.900
-0.003	0.922
0.002	0.936
0.004	0.907
0.009	0.924
0.006	0.915
-0.002	0.883
-0.014	0.957
-0.009	0.960

Source: Y Table 11; Column (8) %.

X Table 9; Column (13).

TABLE A-10

FIVE YEAR AUCTIONS

Independent Variable: NY Acc % Appl

Regression Output:

Constant	-0.0017
Std Err of Y Est	0.0137635
R Squared	0.0012825
No. of Observations	37
Degrees of Freedom	35
Computed "t"	-0.212002
X Coefficient(s)	-0.007099
Std Err of Coef.	0.0334837

Y	X
DAY +1/-1	NY Acc
% CHG	% Appl
0.004	0.380
0.011	0.403
-0.018	0.560
0.001	0.490
-0.053	0.413
-0.001	0.504
0.004	0.399
-0.010	0.446
-0.005	0.531
-0.005	0.496
-0.009	0.464
0.008	0.503
-0.004	0.356
-0.003	0.430
-0.027	0.418
-0.002	0.414
0.002	0.375
0.010	0.386
-0.011	0.448
-0.007	0.317
-0.018	0.298
-0.037	0.396
0.017	0.438
-0.017	0.373
-0.006	0.348
-0.001	0.271
0.002	0.362
0.005	0.425
0.008	0.385
-0.003	0.338
0.002	0.296
0.004	0.343
0.009	0.359
0.006	0.372
-0.002	0.354
-0.014	0.309
-0.009	0.351

Source: Y Table 11; Column (8) %.

X Table 9; Column (15).

APPENDIX B

THIRTY YEAR AUCTION RESULTS:
ALL DATA

TABLE B-1	TABLE B-2

TABLE B-1

THIRTY YEAR AUCTIONS

Independent variable: Coverage Ratio

Regression Output:

Constant	0.2268693
Std Err of Y Est	0.0968834
R Squared	0.2331857
No. of Observations	37
Degrees of Freedom	35
Computed "t"	3.26017
X Coefficient(s)	-0.102576
Std Err of Coef.	0.0314418

Y DAY 0/-1 BP CHG	X Coverage Ratio
-0.08	2.32
0.15	1.82
-0.05	1.66
0.00	1.91
0.21	2.33
-0.13	2.51
-0.11	2.37
0.10	1.54
0.13	2.02
-0.17	2.47
0.12	1.77
0.03	2.04
0.25	2.15
-0.13	2.20
0.01	2.43
0.04	2.15
-0.15	3.47
0.15	1.85
-0.08	2.14
-0.05	2.64
-0.08	2.31
0.02	2.20
-0.03	2.54
-0.17	2.12
-0.01	1.92
-0.03	2.28
-0.04	2.88
-0.12	2.18
-0.10	3.34
-0.12	4.19
0.07	1.98
-0.05	2.55
0.04	2.39
0.17	1.81
-0.05	2.10
-0.04	2.06
0.01	2.03

Source: Y Table 12; Column (7).

X Table 10: Column (5).

TABLE B-2

THIRTY YEAR AUCTIONS

Independent variable: Tail

Regression Output:

Constant	-0.042834
Std Err of Y Est	0.104321
R Squared	0.1109332
No. of Observations	37
Degrees of Freedom	35
Computed "t"	2.1111
X Coefficient(s)	0.0133492
Std Err of Coef.	0.0063879

Y DAY 0/-1 BP CHG	X TAIL
-0.08	3
0.15	6
-0.05	9
0.00	6
0.21	2
-0.13	2
-0.11	2
0.10	14
0.13	5
-0.17	2
0.12	4
0.03	3
0.25	2
-0.13	2
0.01	0
0.04	2
-0.15	0
0.15	4
-0.08	4
-0.05	1
-0.08	2
0.02	2
-0.03	1
-0.17	3
-0.01	2
-0.03	2
-0.04	1
-0.12	1
-0.10	0
-0.12	0
0.07	2
-0.05	1
0.04	1
0.17	4
-0.05	1
-0.04	1
0.01	0

Source: Y Table 12; Column (7).

X Table 10: Column (9).

TABLE B-3

THIRTY YEAR AUCTIONS	
Independent variable: NCmp %	
Regression Output:	
Constant	-0.00331309689
Std Err of Y Est	0.010295413702
R Squared	0.023648357271
No. of Observations	37
Degrees of Freedom	35
Computed "t"	0.9207
X Coefficient(s)	0.024920704945
Std Err of Coef.	0.027066303216

Y	X
DAY 0/-1	NCmp
% CHG	%
-0.007	0.102
0.015	0.091
-0.005	0.077
0.000	0.071
0.017	0.106
-0.009	0.166
-0.008	0.224
0.007	0.090
0.009	0.158
-0.016	0.234
0.011	0.187
0.003	0.213
0.021	0.246
-0.011	0.124
0.001	0.074
0.003	0.078
-0.012	0.061
0.013	0.058
-0.007	0.065
-0.004	0.092
-0.007	0.071
0.002	0.050
-0.003	0.047
-0.023	0.037
-0.001	0.022
-0.004	0.025
-0.005	0.030
-0.014	0.039
-0.011	0.044
-0.013	0.064
0.008	0.037
-0.005	0.054
0.004	0.046
0.019	0.032
-0.005	0.038
-0.005	0.038
0.001	0.034

Source: Table 12; Column (7) %.
X Table 10; Column (11).

TABLE B-4

THIRTY YEAR AUCTIONS	
Independent variable: NYAcc % Ttl	
Regression Output:	
Constant	0.03296056
Std Err of Y Est	0.01033822
R Squared	0.02352632
No. of Observations	34
Degrees of Freedom	32
Computed "t"	-0.878055
X Coefficient(s)	-0.0374148
Std Err of Coef.	0.042611

Y DAY 0/-1 % CHG	X NYAcc as % Ttl
0.000	0.897
0.017	0.886
-0.009	0.871
-0.008	0.795
0.007	0.836
0.009	0.849
-0.016	0.884
0.011	0.894
0.003	0.869
0.021	0.884
-0.011	0.843
0.001	0.938
0.003	0.940
-0.012	0.957
0.013	0.915
-0.007	0.928
-0.004	0.897
-0.007	0.922
0.002	0.942
-0.003	0.955
-0.023	0.949
-0.001	0.947
-0.004	0.942
-0.005	0.946
-0.014	0.960
-0.011	0.944
-0.013	0.950
0.008	0.958
-0.005	0.934
0.004	0.952
0.019	0.948
-0.005	0.933
-0.005	0.951
0.001	0.951

Source: Y Table 12; Column (7) %.

X Table 10; Column (13) .

TABLE B-5

THIRTY YEAR AUCTIONS	
Independent variable: NYAcc % Appl	
Regression Output:	
Constant	-0.0318276
Std Err of Y Est	0.00872691
R Squared	0.30419026
No. of Observations	34
Degrees of Freedom	32
Computed "t"	3.74026515
X Coefficient(s)	0.06578741
Std Err of Coef.	0.01758897

Y DAY 0/-1 % CHG	X NYAcc as % Appl
0.000	0.529
0.017	0.432
-0.009	0.409
-0.008	0.408
0.007	0.663
0.009	0.496
-0.016	0.408
0.011	0.575
0.003	0.516
0.021	0.489
-0.011	0.472
0.001	0.424
0.003	0.504
-0.012	0.305
0.013	0.589
-0.007	0.507
-0.004	0.381
-0.007	0.444
0.002	0.478
-0.003	0.427
-0.023	0.490
-0.001	0.542
-0.004	0.450
-0.005	0.358
-0.014	0.477
-0.011	0.303
-0.013	0.247
0.008	0.527
-0.005	0.401
0.004	0.429
0.019	0.592
-0.005	0.484
-0.005	0.498
0.001	0.508

Source: Y Table 12; Column (7) %.

X Table 10; Column (15).

	TABLE B-6				TABLE B-7	

TABLE B-6

THIRTY YEAR AUCTIONS

Independent Variable: Coverage Ratio

Regression Output:

Constant		0.2131687
Std Err of Y Est		0.1383375
R Squared		0.1257296
No. of Observations		37
Degrees of Freedom		35
Computed "t"	-2.24352	
X Coefficient(s)	-0.100723	
Std Err of Coef.	0.044895	

Y	X
DAY +1/-1	Coverage
BP CHG	Ratio
-0.06	2.32
0.22	1.82
0.17	1.66
0.12	1.91
0.24	2.33
-0.21	2.51
-0.08	2.37
-0.11	1.54
0.02	2.02
-0.24	2.47
0.18	1.77
0.01	2.04
0.2	2.15
-0.14	2.20
0.09	2.43
0.25	2.15
-0.15	3.47
0.03	1.85
-0.1	2.14
-0.19	2.64
-0.1	2.31
0.05	2.20
0.04	2.54
-0.16	2.12
-0.16	1.92
0.05	2.28
-0.04	2.88
-0.14	2.18
-0.18	3.34
-0.07	4.19
-0.03	1.98
-0.11	2.55
0.02	2.39
0.23	1.81
-0.28	2.10
0.01	2.06
-0.02	2.03

Source: Y Table 11; Column (8).

X Table 10; Column (5).

TABLE B-7

THIRTY YEAR AUCTIONS

Independent Variable: Tail

Regression Output:

Constant		-0.051778
Std Err of Y Est		0.1434267
R Squared		0.0602212
No. of Observations		37
Degrees of Freedom		35
Computed "t"	1.4976	
X Coefficient(s)	0.0131526	
Std Err of Coef.	0.0087825	

Y	X
DAY +1/-1	TAIL
BP CHG	
-0.06	3
0.22	6
0.17	9
0.12	6
0.24	2
-0.21	2
-0.08	2
-0.11	14
0.02	5
-0.24	2
0.18	4
0.01	3
0.2	2
-0.14	2
0.09	0
0.25	2
-0.15	0
0.03	4
-0.1	4
-0.19	1
-0.1	2
0.05	2
0.04	1
-0.16	3
-0.16	2
0.05	2
-0.04	1
-0.14	1
-0.18	0
-0.07	0
-0.03	2
-0.11	1
0.02	1
0.23	4
-0.28	1
0.01	1
-0.02	0

Source: Y Table 12; Column (8).

X Table 10; Column (9).

TABLE B-8

THIRTY YEAR AUCTIONS		
Independent Variable: N Cmp %		
Regression Output:		
Constant		-0.00423722286268
Std Err of Y Est		0.014151973539921
R Squared		0.011887843121797
No. of Observations		37
Degrees of Freedom		35
Computed 't'	0.648906961867	
X Coefficient(s)	0.024142630168	
Std Err of Coef.	0.037205071893	

Y DAY +1/-1 % CHG	X NCmp %
-0.005	0.102
0.022	0.091
0.016	0.077
0.010	0.071
0.019	0.106
-0.015	0.166
-0.006	0.224
-0.008	0.090
0.001	0.158
-0.023	0.234
0.016	0.187
0.001	0.213
0.017	0.246
-0.012	0.124
0.008	0.074
0.019	0.078
-0.012	0.061
0.003	0.058
-0.009	0.065
-0.017	0.092
-0.009	0.071
0.005	0.050
0.004	0.047
-0.021	0.037
-0.021	0.022
0.007	0.025
-0.005	0.030
-0.016	0.039
-0.020	0.044
-0.008	0.064
-0.004	0.037
-0.012	0.054
0.002	0.046
0.026	0.032
-0.031	0.038
0.001	0.038
-0.003	0.034

Source: Y Table 12; Column (8) %.

X Table 10; Column (11).

TABLE B-9

THIRTY YEAR AUCTIONS		
Independent Variable: NY Acc % Ttl		
Regression Output:		

Constant		0.00435028
Std Err of Y Est		0.01386468
R Squared		0.000660943
No. of Observations		34
Degrees of Freedom		32
Computed "t"	-0.1454791	
X Coefficient(s)	-0.0083135	
Std Err of Coef.	0.05714599	

Y	X
DAY +1/-1	NY Acc
% CHG	% Ttl
0.010	0.897
0.019	0.886
-0.015	0.871
-0.006	0.795
-0.008	0.836
0.001	0.849
-0.023	0.884
0.016	0.894
0.001	0.869
0.017	0.884
-0.012	0.843
0.008	0.938
0.019	0.940
-0.012	0.957
0.003	0.915
-0.009	0.928
-0.017	0.897
-0.009	0.922
0.005	0.942
0.004	0.955
-0.021	0.949
-0.021	0.947
0.007	0.942
-0.005	0.946
-0.016	0.960
-0.020	0.944
-0.008	0.950
-0.004	0.958
-0.012	0.934
0.002	0.952
0.026	0.948
-0.031	0.933
0.001	0.951
-0.003	0.951

Source: Y Table 12; Column (8) %.

X Table 10; Column (13).

TABLE B-10

THIRTY YEAR AUCTIONS		
Independent Variable: NY Acc % Appl		
Regression Output:		

Constant		-0.0275604
Std Err of Y Est		0.01308541
R Squared		0.10984034
No. of Observations		34
Degrees of Freedom		32
Computed "t"	1.98711026	
X Coefficient(s)	0.05240696	
Std Err of Coef.	0.02637346	

Y	X
DAY +1/-1	NY Acc
% CHG	% Appl
0.010	0.529
0.019	0.432
-0.015	0.409
-0.006	0.408
-0.008	0.663
0.001	0.496
-0.023	0.408
0.016	0.575
0.001	0.516
0.017	0.489
-0.012	0.472
0.008	0.424
0.019	0.504
-0.012	0.305
0.003	0.589
-0.009	0.507
-0.017	0.381
-0.009	0.444
0.005	0.478
0.004	0.427
-0.021	0.490
-0.021	0.542
0.007	0.450
-0.005	0.358
-0.016	0.477
-0.020	0.303
-0.008	0.247
-0.004	0.527
-0.012	0.401
0.002	0.429
0.026	0.592
-0.031	0.484
0.001	0.498
-0.003	0.508

Source: Y Table 12; Column (8) %.

X Table 10; Column (15).

TABLE B-11

THIRTY YEAR AUCTIONS	
Independent Variable: Coverage Ratio	
Regression Output:	
Constant	0.1046218
Std Err of Y Est	0.2101623
R Squared	0.0138003
No. of Observations	37
Degrees of Freedom	35
Computed "t"	-0.699836
X Coefficient(s)	-0.047732
Std Err of Coef.	0.0682044

Y DAY +3/-1 BP CHG	X Coverage Ratio
0.04	2.32
0.10	1.82
0.28	1.66
-0.36	1.91
0.43	2.33
-0.02	2.51
-0.52	2.37
-0.41	1.54
0.39	2.02
-0.09	2.47
0.18	1.77
0.03	2.04
0.22	2.15
-0.11	2.20
0.09	2.43
0.24	2.15
-0.14	3.47
0.15	1.85
-0.06	2.14
-0.32	2.64
0.00	2.31
-0.02	2.20
-0.12	2.54
-0.11	2.12
-0.23	1.92
0.01	2.28
0.10	2.88
-0.03	2.18
0.00	3.34
-0.04	4.19
0.01	1.98
0.00	2.55
0.02	2.39
0.28	1.81
-0.28	2.10
0.07	2.06
0.05	2.03

Source: Y Table 12; Column (9).
X Table 10; Column (5).

TABLE B-12

THIRTY YEAR AUCTIONS	
Independent Variable: NY Acc % Appl	
Regression Output:	
Constant	-0.009403
Std Err of Y Est	0.0182489
R Squared	0.0065154
No. of Observations	34
Degrees of Freedom	32
Computed "t"	0.458106073
X Coefficient(s)	0.016849362
Std Err of Coef.	0.036780482

Y DAY +3/-1 % CHG	X NY Acc % Appl
-0.029	0.529
0.034	0.432
-0.001	0.409
-0.037	0.408
-0.029	0.663
0.027	0.496
-0.008	0.408
0.016	0.575
0.003	0.516
0.019	0.489
-0.009	0.472
0.008	0.424
0.018	0.504
-0.011	0.305
0.013	0.589
-0.005	0.507
-0.028	0.381
0.000	0.444
-0.002	0.478
-0.013	0.427
-0.015	0.490
-0.030	0.542
0.001	0.450
0.013	0.358
-0.003	0.477
0.000	0.303
-0.004	0.247
0.001	0.527
0.000	0.401
0.002	0.429
0.032	0.592
-0.031	0.484
0.009	0.498
0.006	0.508

Source: Y Table 12; Column (9) %.
X Table 10; Column (15).

APPENDIX C

FIVE YEAR AUCTION RESULTS:
EXTREME OBSERVATIONS

TABLE C-1

FIVE YEAR AUCTIONS

Independent variable: Coverage Ratio

Regression Output:

Data points -.5 SD < and > +.5 SD from Mean

Constant	0.0213778
Std Err of Y Est	0.134063
R Squared	0.0072424
No. of Observations	26
Degrees of Freedom	24
Computed "t"	0.4184325
X Coefficient(s)	-0.020042
Std Err of Coef.	0.0478983

Y	X
DAY 0/-1 BP CHG	Coverage Ratio
-0.01	3.50
-0.12	3.35
-0.12	3.34
-0.03	3.24
-0.02	3.22
-0.01	3.04
-0.03	3.02
-0.10	2.97
-0.02	2.97
-0.03	2.93
0.05	2.92
-0.02	2.90
-0.10	2.82
0.03	2.33
-0.10	2.33
-0.06	2.33
-0.07	2.25
-0.05	2.17
-0.06	2.04
0.12	2.03
-0.05	1.99
-0.01	1.99
0.16	1.99
0.42	1.93
-0.31	1.88
-0.25	1.67

Source: Y Table 11; Column (7).
X Table 9: Column (5).

TABLE C-2

FIVE YEAR AUCTIONS

Independent variable: Tail

Regression Output:

Data points -.5 SD < and > +.5 SD from Mean

Constant	-0.066342
Std Err of Y Est	0.1442169
R Squared	0.1715063
No. of Observations	19
Degrees of Freedom	17
Computed "t"	1.875944
X Coefficient(s)	0.0207626
Std Err of Coef.	0.0110678

Y	X
DAY 0/-1 BP CHG	TAIL
0.42	11
-0.25	7
0.16	5
-0.05	4
-0.01	4
-0.08	3
0.12	3
-0.31	3
-0.07	0
-0.10	0
-0.02	0
-0.12	0
-0.01	0
-0.12	0
-0.05	0
-0.04	0
0.01	0
0.05	0
0.04	0

Source: Y Table 11; Column (7).
X Table 9: Column (9).

TABLE C-3		

TABLE C-3

FIVE YEAR AUCTIONS		
Independent variable: NCmp %		
Regression Output:		
Data points -.5 SD < and > +.5 SD from Mean		
Constant		-0.004856
Std Err of Y Est		0.0124128
R Squared		0.0066738
No. of Observations		26
Degrees of Freedom		24
Computed "t"	0.4015554	
X Coefficient(s)	0.0145029	
Std Err of Coef.	0.0361167	

Y	X	
DAY 0/-1	NCmp	
% CHG	%	
-0.0047	0.2272	
0.0103	0.2211	
-0.0066	0.1845	
0.0037	0.1833	
-0.0421	0.1764	
-0.0059	0.1755	
-0.0176	0.1723	
0.0037	0.1704	
-0.0010	0.1656	
0.0100	0.1507	
-0.0036	0.1483	
0.0182	0.1470	
0.0140	0.1377	
-0.0022	0.0734	
-0.0018	0.0709	
-0.0171	0.0598	
0.0071	0.0465	
-0.0144	0.0437	
0.0061	0.0436	
-0.0131	0.0435	
-0.0013	0.0421	
0.0012	0.0388	
-0.0038	0.0339	
-0.0044	0.0322	
-0.0151	0.0319	
-0.0045	0.0308	

Source: Table 11; Column (7) %.

X Table 9; Column (11).

TABLE C-4

FIVE YEAR AUCTIONS		
Independent variable: NYAcc % Ttl		
Regression Output:		
Data points -.5 SD < and > +.5 SD from Mean		
Constant		0.0008022
Std Err of Y Est		0.0082129
R Squared		0.0010646
No. of Observations		23
Degrees of Freedom		21
Computed "t"	-0.149601	
X Coefficient(s)	-0.003605	
Std Err of Coef.	0.0241006	

Y	X	
DAY 0/-1	NYAcc	
% CHG	as % Ttl	
-0.0038	0.9595	
0.0061	0.9593	
-0.0144	0.9568	
-0.0045	0.9454	
-0.0151	0.9374	
-0.0011	0.9363	
0.0071	0.9337	
-0.0088	0.9274	
-0.0022	0.9240	
-0.0013	0.9223	
-0.0131	0.9164	
-0.0031	0.9163	
-0.0044	0.9161	
0.0042	0.9145	
0.0140	0.8455	
0.0037	0.8432	
-0.0010	0.8264	
-0.0050	0.8220	
0.0037	0.8050	
0.0100	0.8041	
-0.0036	0.8008	
-0.0044	0.7383	
-0.0176	0.7175	

Source: Y Table 11; Column (7) %.
X Table 9; Column (13).

TABLE C-5

FIVE YEAR AUCTIONS

Independent variable: NYAcc % Appl

Regression Output:

Data Points -.5 SD < and > +.5 SD from Mean

Constant	-0.0057309
Std Err of Y Est	0.00706365
R Squared	0.00358269
No. of Observations	23
Degrees of Freedom	21
Computed "t"	0.00011698
X Coefficient(s)	0.00479625
Std Err of Coef.	0.01745454

Y	X
DAY 0/-1	NYAcc
% CHG	as % Appl
-0.0176	0.5595
-0.0059	0.5313
-0.0036	0.5042
0.0103	0.5034
-0.0010	0.4962
0.0100	0.4900
-0.0066	0.4639
-0.0050	0.4477
-0.0047	0.4461
-0.0131	0.4384
0.0061	0.3619
-0.0022	0.3591
-0.0088	0.3563
0.0011	0.3538
-0.0038	0.3513
-0.0045	0.3479
-0.0022	0.3425
-0.0013	0.3384
-0.0021	0.3169
-0.0144	0.3095
-0.0130	0.2983
-0.0011	0.2959
-0.0044	0.2710

Source: Y Table 11; Column (7) %.

X Table 9; Column (15).

TABLE C-6

FIVE YEAR AUCTIONS

Independent Variable: Tail

Regression Output:

Data Points -.5 SD < and > +.5 SD from Mean

Constant	-0.0692002
Std Err of Y Est	0.18011816
R Squared	0.03827606
No. of Observations	19
Degrees of Freedom	17
Computed "t"	0.82255102
X Coefficient(s)	0.01137012
Std Err of Coef.	0.01382299

Y	X
DAY +1/-1	TAIL
BP CHG	
0.38	11
-0.25	7
0.02	5
-0.02	4
-0.05	4
-0.38	3
0.09	3
-0.42	3
-0.09	0
-0.05	0
0.04	0
-0.17	0
0.02	0
-0.12	0
0.11	0
-0.03	0
-0.02	0
0.02	0
0.06	0

Source: Y Table 11; Column (8).

X Table 9; Column (9).

APPENDIX D

THIRTY YEAR AUCTION RESULTS: EXTREME OBSERVATIONS

TABLE D-1	TABLE D-2

THIRTY YEAR AUCTIONS

Independent variable: Coverage Ratio

Regression Output:

Data points -.5 SD < and > +.5 SD from Me

Constant		0.2635316
Std Err of Y Est		0.0680901
R Squared		0.5906634
No. of Observations		17
Degrees of Freedom		15
Computed "t"	4.6523824	
X Coefficient(s)	-0.105409	
Std Err of Coef.	0.022657	

Y	X
DAY 0/-1 BP CHG	Coverage Ratio
-0.12	4.19
-0.15	3.47
-0.10	3.34
-0.04	2.88
-0.05	2.64
-0.05	2.55
0.01	2.03
0.13	2.02
0.07	1.98
-0.01	1.92
0.00	1.91
0.15	1.85
0.15	1.82
0.17	1.81
0.12	1.77
-0.05	1.66
0.10	1.54

Source: Y Table 12; Column (7).
X Table 10: Column (5).

THIRTY YEAR AUCTIONS

Independent variable: Tail

Regression Output:

Data points -.5 SD < and > +.5 SD from Me

Constant		-0.040308
Std Err of Y Est		0.0862899
R Squared		0.2509106
No. of Observations		22
Degrees of Freedom		20
Computed "t"	2.588259	
X Coefficient(s)	0.0138558	
Std Err of Coef.	0.0053533	

Y	X
DAY 0/-1 BP CHG	TAIL
0.10	14
-0.05	9
0.15	6
0.00	6
0.13	5
-0.08	4
0.12	4
0.17	4
0.15	4
-0.04	1
-0.05	1
-0.03	1
-0.04	1
-0.05	1
-0.12	1
-0.05	1
0.04	1
-0.12	0
-0.15	0
-0.10	0
0.01	0
0.01	0

Source: Y Table 12; Column (7)
X Table 10: Column (9)

TABLE D-3

THIRTY YEAR AUCTIONS		
Independent variable: NCmp %		
Regression Output:		
Data points -.5 SD < and > +.5 SD from Mean		
Constant		-0.003822
Std Err of Y Est		0.0108327
R Squared		0.0258913
No. of Observations		23
Degrees of Freedom		21
Computed "t"	0.7471077	
X Coefficient(s)	0.0216288	
Std Err of Coef.	0.02895	

Y	X	
DAY 0/-1	NCmp	
% CHG	%	
0.0211	0.2456	
-0.0160	0.2335	
-0.0078	0.2240	
0.0029	0.2132	
0.0110	0.1870	
-0.0093	0.1664	
0.0090	0.1576	
-0.0110	0.1241	
-0.0054	0.0543	
0.0020	0.0503	
-0.0032	0.0473	
0.0044	0.0458	
-0.0112	0.0441	
-0.0137	0.0390	
-0.0055	0.0385	
-0.0049	0.0384	
-0.0226	0.0374	
0.0083	0.0373	
0.0013	0.0340	
0.0193	0.0323	
-0.0053	0.0301	
-0.0040	0.0246	
-0.0013	0.0217	

Source: Table 12; Column (7) %.
X Table 10; Column (11).

TABLE D-4

THIRTY YEAR AUCTIONS		
Independent variable: NYAcc % Ttl		
Regression Output:		
Data points -.5 SD < and > +.5 SD from Mean		
Constant		0.0303437
Std Err of Y Est		0.0111631
R Squared		0.0211527
No. of Observations		27
Degrees of Freedom		25
Computed "t"	-0.74	
X Coefficient(s)	-0.0343	
Std Err of Coef.	0.0466	

Y	X	
DAY 0/-1	NYAcc	
% CHG	as % Ttl	
-0.0137	0.9596	
0.0083	0.9576	
-0.0119	0.9570	
-0.0032	0.9547	
0.0044	0.9521	
0.0013	0.9513	
-0.0049	0.9510	
-0.0135	0.9500	
-0.0226	0.9487	
0.0193	0.9478	
-0.0013	0.9474	
-0.0053	0.9460	
-0.0112	0.9444	
-0.0040	0.9423	
0.0020	0.9417	
0.0030	0.9397	
0.0008	0.9376	
0.0110	0.8937	
0.0168	0.8861	
0.0211	0.8839	
-0.0160	0.8838	
-0.0093	0.8714	
0.0029	0.8687	
0.0090	0.8491	
-0.0110	0.8434	
0.0072	0.8357	
-0.0078	0.7954	

Source: Y Table 12; Column (7) %.
X Table 10; Column (13).

TABLE D-5

THIRTY YEAR AUCTIONS
Independent variable: NYAcc % Appl
Regression Output:
Data Points -.5 SD < and > +.5 SD from Mean

Constant		-0.03448
Std Err of Y Est		0.005583
R Squared		0.691926
No. of Observations		19
Degrees of Freedom		17
Computed "t"	6.1791258	
X Coefficient(s)	0.0712674	
Std Err of Coef.	0.0115336	

Y DAY 0/-1 % CHG	X NYAcc as % Appl
0.0072	0.6626
0.0193	0.5917
0.0129	0.5893
0.0110	0.5747
-0.0013	0.5418
0.0000	0.5292
0.0083	0.5273
0.0029	0.5163
0.0013	0.5083
-0.0070	0.5071
-0.0093	0.4089
-0.0160	0.4080
-0.0078	0.4076
-0.0054	0.4006
-0.0044	0.3809
-0.0053	0.3584
-0.0119	0.3047
-0.0112	0.3031
-0.0135	0.2467

Source: Y Table 12; Column (7) %.

X Table 10; Column (15).

TABLE D-6

THIRTY YEAR AUCTIONS
Independent Variable: Coverage Ratio
Regression Output:
Data Points -.5 SD < and > +.5 SD from Mean

Constant		0.235062
Std Err of Y Est		0.123597
R Squared		0.298017
No. of Observations		17
Degrees of Freedom		15
Computed "t"	2.5234995	
X Coefficient(s)	-0.103784	
Std Err of Coef.	0.041127	

Y DAY +1/-1 BP CHG	X Coverage Ratio
-0.07	4.19
-0.15	3.47
-0.18	3.34
-0.04	2.88
-0.19	2.64
-0.11	2.55
-0.02	2.03
0.02	2.02
-0.03	1.98
-0.16	1.92
0.12	1.91
0.03	1.85
0.22	1.82
0.23	1.81
0.18	1.77
0.17	1.66
-0.11	1.54

Source: Y Table 11; Column (8).

X Table 10; Column (5).

TABLE D-7

THIRTY YEAR AUCTIONS		
Independent Variable: Tail		
Regression Output:		
Data points -.5 SD < and > +.5 SD from Mean		

Constant		-0.0516
Std Err of Y Est		0.13543
R Squared		0.11715
No. of Observations		22
Degrees of Freedom		20
Computed "t"	1.6290831	
X Coefficient(s)	0.0136879	
Std Err of Coef.	0.0084022	

Y DAY +1/-1 BP CHG	X TAIL
-0.11	14
0.17	9
0.22	6
0.12	6
0.02	5
-0.10	4
0.18	4
0.23	4
0.03	4
0.01	1
-0.11	1
0.04	1
-0.04	1
-0.19	1
-0.14	1
-0.28	1
0.02	1
-0.07	0
-0.15	0
-0.18	0
0.09	0
-0.02	0

Source: Y Table 12; Column (8).

X Table 10; Column (9).

TABLE D-8

THIRTY YEAR AUCTIONS		
Independent Variable: NY Acc % Appl		
Regression Output:		
Data points -.5 SD < and > +.5 SD from Mean		

Constant		-0.0329
Std Err of Y Est		0.01104
R Squared		0.28482
No. of Observations		19
Degrees of Freedom		17
Computed "t"	2.6019431	
X Coefficient(s)	0.0593264	
Std Err of Coef.	0.0228008	

Y DAY +1/-1 % CHG	X NY Acc as%Appl
-0.0079	0.6626
0.0261	0.5917
0.0026	0.5893
0.0165	0.5747
-0.0211	0.5418
0.0095	0.5292
-0.0036	0.5273
0.0010	0.5163
-0.0025	0.5083
-0.0088	0.5071
-0.0150	0.4089
-0.0226	0.4080
-0.0057	0.4076
-0.0119	0.4006
-0.0167	0.3809
-0.0053	0.3584
-0.0119	0.3047
-0.0201	0.3031
-0.0078	0.2467

Source: Y Table 12; Column (8) %.
X Table 10; Column (11).

TABLE D-9	TABLE D-10

THIRTY YEAR AUCTIONS

Independent Variable: Coverage Ratio

Regression Output:

Data points -.5 SD < and > +.5 SD from Mean

Constant	0.10608331
Std Err of Y Est	0.23697923
R Squared	0.02105573
No. of Observations	17
Degrees of Freedom	15
Computed "t"	0.568004522
X Coefficient(s)	-0.04479003
Std Err of Coef.	0.078855055

Y	X
DAY +3/-1 BP CHG	Coverage Ratio
-0.04	4.19
-0.14	3.47
0.00	3.34
0.10	2.88
-0.32	2.64
0.00	2.55
0.05	2.03
0.39	2.02
0.01	1.98
-0.23	1.92
-0.36	1.91
0.15	1.85
0.10	1.82
0.28	1.81
0.18	1.77
0.28	1.66
-0.41	1.54

Source: Y Table 11; Column (9).
X Table 10; Column (5).

THIRTY YEAR AUCTIONS

Independent Variable: Tail

Regression Output:

Data points -.5 SD < and > +.5 SD from Mean

Constant	0.0094227
Std Err of Y Est	0.2137741
R Squared	0.0045736
No. of Observations	22
Degrees of Freedom	20
Computed "t"	-0.303136
X Coefficient(s)	-0.0040203
Std Err of Coef.	0.01326234

Y	X
DAY +3/-1 BP CHG	TAIL
-0.41	14
0.28	9
0.10	6
-0.36	6
0.39	5
-0.06	4
0.18	4
0.28	4
0.15	4
0.07	1
0.00	1
-0.12	1
0.10	1
-0.32	1
-0.03	1
-0.28	1
0.02	1
-0.04	0
-0.14	0
0.00	0
0.09	0
0.05	0

Source: Y Table 12; Column (9).
X Table 10; Column (9).

TABLE D-11

THIRTY YEAR AUCTIONS	
Independent Variable: NY Acc % Appl	
Regression Output:	
Data points -.5 SD < and > +.5 SD from Mean	

Constant	-0.0126023
Std Err of Y Est	0.0189171
R Squared	0.00977454
No. of Observations	19
Degrees of Freedom	17
Computed "t"	0.40964294
X Coefficient(s)	0.016008067
Std Err of Coef.	0.039078098

Y	X
DAY +3/-1	NY Acc
% CHG	as%.Appl
-0.0294	0.6626
0.0317	0.5917
0.0129	0.5893
0.0165	0.5747
-0.0304	0.5418
-0.0286	0.5292
0.0012	0.5273
0.0029	0.5163
0.0063	0.5083
-0.0053	0.5071
-0.0014	0.4089
-0.0085	0.4080
-0.0367	0.4076
0.0000	0.4006
-0.0281	0.3809
0.0133	0.3584
-0.0111	0.3047
0.0000	0.3031
-0.0045	0.2467

Source: Y Table 12; Column (9) %.
X Table 10: Column (11).

INDEX